THE MAKING
OF COMMUNITY

THE MAKING OF COMMUNITY

ACTS 1 TO 12 / KEVIN GILES

AN ALBATROSS BOOK

the bible reading fellowship
OPENING THE BIBLE

© Commentary: Kevin Giles 1992
© Discussion questions: Albatross Books Pty Ltd 1992

Published in Australia and New Zealand by
Albatross Books Pty Ltd
PO Box 320, Sutherland
NSW 2232, Australia
in the United States of America by
Albatross Books
PO Box 131, Claremont
CA 91711, USA
and in the United Kingdom by
The Bible Reading Fellowship
Peter's Way, Sandy Lane West
Oxford OX4 5HG, England

First edition 1992
Reprinted 1993

This book is copyright. Apart from any fair dealing for the purposes of private study, research, criticism or review as permitted under the Copyright Act, no part of this book may be reproduced by any process without the written permission of the publisher.

National Library of Australia
Cataloguing-in-Publication data

Kevin Giles
The Making of Community

ISBN 0 86760 147 7 (Albatross)
ISBN 0 7459 2188 4 (BRF)

1. Bible. N.T. Acts I–XII — Commentaries.
I. Title

225.607

Cover photo: Kathryn Mollenhauer
Printed and bound in Australia by McPherson's Printing Group, Victoria

Contents

Introduction	7
1 Preparation for the community ACTS CHAPTER 1	24
2 The founding of the community ACTS CHAPTER 2	36
3 Membership of the community ACTS CHAPTER 3	50
4 Signs of trouble in the community ACTS CHAPTER 4	65
5 Threats from without and within ACTS CHAPTER 5	77
6 Leadership in the new community ACTS CHAPTER 6	88
7 A spirited defence of the community's beliefs ACTS CHAPTER 7	99
8 The spreading of the gospel ACTS CHAPTER 8	109

9 A dramatic entry into the faith
ACTS CHAPTER 9
119

10 Launching the Gentile mission
ACTS CHAPTERS 10 AND
11, VERSES 1 TO 18
128

11 Establishing the Gentile church
ACTS CHAPTER 11, VERSES 19 TO 30
141

12 Growth despite the odds
ACTS CHAPTER 12
154

Endnotes *165*
Bibliography *169*

Introduction

THE ACTS OF THE APOSTLES is arguably the most exciting and interesting book in the New Testament. It tells of the adventures of the earliest Christians in the years immediately following the ministry, death and resurrection of Jesus. Here we read the account of the new Christians first receiving the power of the Holy Spirit, of mass conversions, of early congregational squabbles and of the first steps in establishing local church communities.

Great leaders such as Peter, Stephen, Philip, Barnabas and Paul are introduced. The triumph of the gospel in Jerusalem, Judea, Samaria, Antioch in Syria and then in the cities of Asia Minor, Greece and Italy are recounted. If we did not have this book, we would simply not have this information.

In these studies, only the first twelve chapters of Acts are covered. All the above people or events, excepting the remarkable missionary exploits of Paul, are dealt with. Chapter 12 is a good point to make a break, for the focus changes at this point. In chapter 13, the worldwide mission begins and Paul becomes the main character in the drama which follows.

The author

The third Gospel, the Gospel of Luke, and the Book of Acts were written by one person. They are both addressed to Theophilus. The opening verse of Acts says that what follows continues the story from 'the first book' of 'what Jesus began to do and teach', and the writing style and the theological outlook of the two books are the same.

The author nowhere gives his name but, from earliest times, the third Gospel and Acts have been ascribed to Luke, the friend and companion of Paul. Mentioned by name three times in the New Testament,[1] he probably wrote shortly before AD 70, as he does not mention Paul's martyrdom under Nero (AD 54-68) or the fall of Jerusalem (AD 70).

Luke was not one of the original followers of Jesus, but an early non-Jewish — or Gentile — convert. According to early tradition, he came from the city of Antioch. He had an excellent mastery of the Greek language, but was equally conversant with Jewish thought.

It has often been suggested that Luke writes especially for Gentiles but, as we will see, Luke drew heavily on the rich heritage of the Old Testament to explain who Jesus is and why the gospel was being offered to Gentiles. Non-Jews, without a good knowledge of Judaism, simply would not have seen the force of arguments drawn from the Old Testament.

A more plausible idea is that Luke wrote hoping to reach both enquirers about Christianity and young converts, some being of Jewish and others of Gentile origins — the Gentiles being closely associated with Judaism. Such Gentiles, before considering or becoming Christians, were converts to Judaism or 'God-fearers' — Gentile sympathisers who had not accepted the full yoke of the Law.

Important themes and topics

Luke wrote both as an historian and a theologian (see below for more on this). He wanted to outline what happened and explain why God acted in certain ways. Thus, as his story unfolds, we note that Luke was at pains to emphasise certain matters and to develop a number of themes or, to put it more technically, *theological motifs*.

It is important to highlight some of these so that, what at first thought might seem to be an incidental event or isolated comment, is recognised as part of a bigger picture.

❑ *God the Holy Spirit*

A recent book by Roger Stronstad is entitled *The Charismatic Theology of St Luke*.[2] Stronstad correctly argues that Luke's interest in the Holy Spirit governs his writing. It has even been argued from quite early times that the traditional title, 'The Acts of the Apostles', is a misnomer. Only one of the twelve apostles, Peter, and only one missionary apostle, Paul, is given any prominence. Rather, the central character and unifying theme is the Holy Spirit. The suggestion thus has been made that this book should be called 'The Acts of the Holy Spirit'.

Luke speaks of the Spirit in personal terms and equates him with God (in Acts 5, verses 3 and 4), but he says far more about what the Spirit *does* than who he is. The Spirit works in the following ways:

* *The Spirit empowers*
In his sermon on the day of Pentecost, Peter argues that the prophecy of Joel, which tells what would happen on the last days, has been fulfilled. The Spirit is now given to all God's people (chapter 2, verses 17 and 18). In the Old Testament age, the Spirit only came upon prophets, kings or other special people and then often only for a limited period. In these last days, Luke teaches, the Spirit is given permanently to all believers. In his view, you cannot be a Christian unless you have the Holy Spirit. This gift from God, Luke insists (Luke 24, verse 9 and Acts 1, verse 8), is a life-transforming power.

* *The Spirit guides*
In Acts, the Holy Spirit directs the mission. It is

the Spirit who, among other things, leads Philip to preach to the Ethiopian eunuch, who tells Peter that Cornelius' servants are coming for him, who commands Peter to go with these Gentiles and who reveals to Agabas that a famine is coming.[3]

✻ *The Spirit provides leaders*
Luke suggests that all the leaders in the early church were Spirit-filled persons. They were raised up and empowered by the Holy Spirit. The apostles are said to have been chosen by the Spirit and filled with the Spirit (chapter 1, verses 3 and 5; chapter 9, verse 17; chapter 11, verse 24). The Seven, similarly, are described as 'full of the Spirit and of wisdom'. Barnabas is surnamed 'son of encouragement', the Greek word being a form of one of the titles for the Holy Spirit in John's Gospel.[4]

The most prominent church leaders in Acts, after the apostles, are the prophets. These men and women are made ministers of the word by the Holy Spirit. The elders, who are community leaders with general oversight of local groups of Christians, are also said to be given their ministry by the Holy Spirit.[5]

❏ *Salvation*
In both the third Gospel and Acts, Luke makes the

offer of salvation — our rescue — the heart of the Christian message. Scottish theologian Professor I.H. Marshall argues that 'salvation is the central motif in Lucan theology'. This is suggested by Luke's frequent use of the term 'salvation' or its equivalents, and by the numerous stories which tell of people or groups who receive salvation as the message is proclaimed. In Acts, the many sermons given in a missionary situation conclude with a call to repentance and faith. These sermons, says Professor van Unnik, have one theme: 'the need of salvation, the Man of salvation, the way of salvation'.

In Acts, this salvation is offered to all — Jew and Gentile. It is received, according to Acts 20, verse 21, on the basis of repentance of sins and faith in Christ. Some twenty-nine times, Luke uses the verb 'to believe', usually in the Greek aorist tense, which indicates that believing is a once-for-all decision. Those who repent and believe are given the Holy Spirit and baptised in water.[6] The *content* of this salvation, then, is the gift of the Holy Spirit and the forgiveness of sins.[7]

❑ *Jew and Gentile*

In offering salvation to Gentiles, a radical breach was made with the historic faith of Israel by the early missionaries. We forget today what a divisive and momentous step this was. The reading of Acts, however, brings this fact to the fore. Luke is at pains to show how and why Gentiles come to be offered the salvation once reserved for Jews.

Jesus' own mission was almost entirely directed to Jews and only in his final, post-resurrection charge (recorded in Matthew 28, verse 29 and Luke 24, verse 47) did he command his disciples to go into the whole world and preach the gospel.

As an historian, Luke tells how the mission to Gentiles began and, as a theologian, he gives the reasons. He develops his case step by step:

* Luke insists that the gospel was offered first of all to Jews and the first recipients of the salvation found in Christ (in Acts 2 to 6) were all Jews.[8] The Jewish Christians are thus the foundation on which Gentile believers were added.
* Only reluctantly and slowly was this offer of salvation extended to Samaritans (heretical Jews) and 'God-fearers' ('half-converted' Jews) — and then to Gentiles only by the direct command of God to Peter, recorded in Acts 8.
* Luke argues that the Gentile mission began because of God's direct leading, but he adds that the Jews themselves helped initiate this radical departure by rejecting the gospel first offered to them. Because they refused to repent and believe, he speaks of them being cut off from the people of God and of characteristically opposing the Holy Spirit (Acts 3, verse 23; Acts 7, verse 26).
* Finally, Luke argues that this departure is according to prophecy. In God's eternal plan, first

revealed to the Old Testament prophets, the inclusion of Gentiles is foreshadowed.[9]

What Luke therefore describes is a progressive development rather than a radical breach with the past. The Christian community grows out of Israel, taking with it believing Jews and adding believing Gentiles. In Luke's mind, the Christians are those who recognise that Jesus is the Jewish Messiah and who have been brought to life by the Holy Spirit. They are the Spirit-filled people of God, the community of salvation and, as such, the restored Israel of the last days.

❑ *Christian community life*

In Acts, there are numerous comments about Christian community life. Most of them describe matters quite foreign to our own experience of church. But because they are different, we should not try to make them fit our modern conceptions. It is important that we hear and accept what Luke himself is saying and recognise that church life today is the product of two thousand years of church history.

In Acts, the early Christians celebrated the Lord's Supper or eucharist in a home setting, calling it (in Acts 2, verses 42 and 46) 'the breaking of bread'. Probably the head of the home presided, for ordained ministers were not known. Water baptism is closely associated with becoming a Christian, but it is not directly tied with Spirit baptism or receiving the Spirit — two expressions that mean the same for

Luke. People can be baptised in water and not receive the Spirit, or they can receive the Spirit before they are baptised in water.[10]

At first, the apostles were the leaders of the Christians and their chief teachers but, with the passing of time, Luke allowed that older men — elders — took over as communal leaders, while prophets became the teachers and ministers. If anyone was in need, those who were better off gave freely. The care of widows was a special concern.[11]

The Christian community can be named in many ways. The word 'church' is only one of Luke's collective titles. Others are 'the disciples', 'the brethren', (less commonly) 'followers of the way', 'the saints', 'Christians', 'those who believe' and 'those who call on the name' [of Jesus].[12]

In Acts, we catch a glimpse of Christian community life guided and directed by the Spirit before institutional forms and patterns have in any major way become established.

Going into things further: Luke as historian, theologian and literary artist

A great awakening of interest in the writings of Luke began as a result of a book written in 1953 by a German New Testament scholar, Hans Conzelmann, and published in English in 1960 under the title *The Theology of St Luke*[13]. Conzelmann argued that Luke should not be understood as an historian, as most scholars up to this time had assumed, but rather as a theologian who was reinterpreting the gospel message for the second generation of Christians.

According to Conzelmann, Luke had come to accept that Jesus was not about to return and so he played down the teaching on the near return of Christ and the inbreaking of the kingdom of God, emphasising instead that the present was 'the age of the church', a long epoch, part of God's ongoing work in history. Conzelmann's thesis was radical: its most obvious merit was that he had picked up some things hitherto unseen.

At first it seemed as if he would carry most other scholars with him but, as work began on the numerous details which made up his sweeping proposal, the superstructure and then the foundation began to crumble. Journal articles, monographs and books were written in answer. Luke-Acts became, as a learned professor wrote, 'one of the storm centres of New Testament scholarship'.

Conzelmann's understanding of Luke's motives and his specific arguments were in the main refuted, but in the process Luke was discovered as an individual theological voice within the New Testament. In any study now of New Testament theology, we do not only ask what Jesus said, or Paul or John taught, but also what Luke taught.

In this study, Luke's theological contribution will constantly be highlighted. We will be on the lookout for the special ways Luke explains things and for the matters he emphasises. We will discover that he has some quite original ideas about the twelve apostles, the Holy Spirit, salvation, Jew and Gentile, the Christian community, the dignity of women, the use of possessions and many other matters.

In highlighting Luke's theology, it is not being suggested that Luke is in opposition to other New Testament writers. The point is rather that this focus underlines the fact that the New Testament is the record of *many* witnesses to the apostolic faith, each complementing the other. When the four Gospels are superficially harmonised, or the book of Acts is explained in terms of Paul's theology, then something of the rich diversity of the New Testament revelation is lost. Conzelmann may have been wrong in detail, but for the discovery of Luke the theologian, with some additional points to say on his own account, we have to give this provocative German scholar most of the thanks.

The new emphasis on Luke the theologian is helpful, but we must not forget that Luke is also a good historian. The traditional understanding of Luke is correct, even if it was one-sided. Luke, more than any other writer in the New Testament, shows how secular history and salvation history are related. He attempts to carefully date the birth of Jesus (Luke 2, verses 1 to 3) and the commencement of his ministry (Luke 3, verses 1 and 2) and one of the special features of Acts is the numerous references to historical places, persons and events. These details Luke normally gets right.

At the turn of the century, Professor Sir William Ramsey, a great British historian, made this point about Luke's accuracy very forcibly in several works. As a young man, he had studied in Germany and accepted many radically liberal ideas, one of which was that Acts was a second century fictitious story.

In his archaeological work in Asia Minor in later years, he was forced to abandon this thesis because he found the book of Acts was an amazingly accurate account which could only have been written by someone intimately conversant with the events, people and places he was writing about. Professor Ramsey tells how he changed his mind in his book, *St Paul the Traveller and Roman Citizen*. One of his memorable lines was: 'it was gradually borne in upon me that in various details, the narrative [of Acts] showed marvellous truth.'[14]

It is important also to note that Luke is what has been called a biographical historian. He tells his story, especially in Acts where he is the master of his material, mainly by highlighting the activities of a few key players. The 'big six' are Peter, Stephen, Philip, Paul, Barnabas and James the brother of Jesus. Only one of these, Peter, is one of the twelve apostles.

We thus see again the limitation of calling Luke's second volume by the traditional title, 'The Acts of the Apostles', unless by this we mean the acts of the apostles Peter and Paul. It is certainly not the story of the activities of the twelve. Our present title for Luke's second volume is first found late in the second century AD.

But besides being a careful historian and a good theologian, Luke is also a clever literary artist. This is seen in several ways. He is able to vary his style to suit the story he is telling. For instance, he writes the prologue to his Gospel addressed to Theophilus in perfect classical Greek prose, but then goes on to record the infancy stories adopting the style of the Greek Old Testament.

This gift is seen even more forcibly in his tendency to balance different parts of his unfolding drama. He writes so that the Gospel story and the Acts story often run in parallel. There are many examples, some of which are the following: both the Gospel and Acts begin with a prologue addressed to Theophilus; both tell of introductory events before the Spirit is given on the one hand to Jesus and on the other to the first disciples (Luke 1 to 3; Acts 1 and 2); Jesus' ministry begins with a sermon and so does Peter's (Luke 4; Acts 2); Jesus travels to Jerusalem to be arrested and so does Paul (Luke 9, verse 51 onwards; Acts 19, verse 23 onwards); Jesus is put on trial in Jerusalem but declared innocent three times and so is Paul (Luke 22, verse 26 onwards; Luke 23, verses 4, 14 and 22; Acts 23, verse 24 onwards; Acts 23, verse 9; Acts 25, verse 25; and Acts 26, verse 31.)

But not only are there parallels between the Gospel and Acts, and Jesus and Paul, but also Luke develops parallels between 'the acts of Peter' (Acts

1 to 12) and the 'acts of Paul' (Acts 13 to 26). The significance of these parallels is much discussed. They are certainly an aspect of Luke's theology. In part at least, Luke is arguing that there is a consistent, typical pattern in God's unfolding work in history. The Acts story is the continuation of the Gospel story: Peter and the other apostles continue the work of Jesus; Paul complements the work of Peter.

Discussion questions

Talking it through

1 Acts is arguably the most exciting book in the New Testament. What makes it this for you?

2 If the book of Acts is really the 'Acts of the Holy Spirit', what part does the Holy Spirit play in *our* lives?

3 Unpack the technical word 'salvation'. Can you think of an everyday example that explains this word?

4 How was the Christian church in Acts different from the church today?

22/Introduction

Widening our horizons

1 Luke wrote Acts as a history of the early church based on his own experience. If you were to write a history based on your own experience, what would you aim to do?

2 What do you think 'salvation of the whole person' means? How would such salvation affect your attitude to:
(a) accumulating as many possessions as possible
(b) spending months looking after a dying relative
(c) giving money to World Vision or some similar aid organisation.

3 The early Christians were dragged kicking and screaming into accepting Gentiles into the church. Why are such changes difficult? Are the following contemporary situations similar or not:
(a) accepting women into church leadership
(b) having a racially desegregated church
(c) welcoming homosexuals into church?

4 A community like the New Testament church has a lot of advantages. How can each of the following be made a real community:
(a) your church
(b) your family
(c) your neighbourhood
(d) a group that shares a common interest with you?

Would you see advantages in this? Any disadvantages?

1
Preparation for the community

ACTS CHAPTER 1

IN THIS FIRST CHAPTER, Luke wants to set the scene and answer immediate questions. The Gospels end with Jesus resurrected and alive. The early Christian community would have wanted to know more of what happened after that. Luke writes to meet this need, beginning just where the Gospels conclude.

Luke indicates that the work of the Holy Spirit is crucial to the establishment of the Christian community. It cannot begin until the Spirit is poured out on the disciples. This chapter prepares us for this just as the birth stories in Luke's Gospel prepare for the beginning of Jesus' ministry. The steps in preparing for the founding of the community by the Holy Spirit are that Jesus is to give final instructions to the apostles, ascend into heaven and a twelfth apostle appointed. These are the things we read about in this introductory chapter.

Setting the scene (verses 1 to 5)

In verses 1 and 2 of Acts, Luke tells Theophilus that 'in the first book' he has 'dealt with all that Jesus began to do and teach'. In other words, the Gospel of Luke relates the beginning of Jesus' ministry. The book of Acts, on the other hand, tells of the continuation of Jesus' work as the living, active, risen Lord of the church.

In verses 2 to 5 of this prologue, Luke introduces a number of key ideas which will play an important part in the unfolding drama. First, we are told of the appearances of the resurrected Jesus to his disciples over a forty-day period(verses 2 and 3). While these came to an end when he ascended into heaven, Jesus as their risen Lord continued to be a real presence in the lives of the early Christians.

Second, Luke says Jesus spoke to the apostles 'whom he had chosen' (verse 2) about the kingdom of God. Some of these apostles were to play key roles in Acts in spreading this kingdom .

Finally, Jesus' promise of the coming of the Holy Spirit is stressed(verse 5). John's baptism with water is contrasted with a pivotal feature of Acts, the anticipated baptism with the Holy Spirit.

26/Preparation for the community

Final instructions (verses 6 to 11)

As Luke begins the narrative proper, he uses a confused question put to Jesus by the disciples to present some important information. The disciples ask, 'Lord, will you at this time restore the kingdom to Israel?' The question shows that the disciples are still hoping for the establishment of a triumphant Jewish national state ruled by the Messiah. Even at this point they have not fully grasped the radical nature of Jesus' mission. It is the offer of the gospel to Jew and Gentile *alike*.

The importance of the Jewish nation in the unfolding plan of God at this point is transitional — the offer will first be made to Jews and the Jews who believe will begin the church, but then the gospel will go to Gentiles and eventually they will predominate in the church.

Luke does not have Jesus answer this question directly. He first tells the apostles in verse 8 that it is not for them to know the times and the seasons when God will act in history, but rather they are to prepare themselves for the coming of the Holy Spirit. This will empower them as witnesses in Jerusalem, Judea, Samaria and to the ends of the earth. The mission begins in the holy city, moves throughout Judea and Samaria, but has as its ultimate goal the whole world. Jewish particularism is to be replaced by a universal offer of salvation.

As far as Luke and the other New Testament writers are concerned, the exaltation of Jesus to sit at God's right hand, the place of authority, follows immediately after the resurrection. The resurrection and the exaltation are but two steps in the one movement.[1]

Luke, however, adds a unique account, given twice, of Jesus' *final departure from earth* after forty days of bodily resurrection appearances — at the end of his Gospel (Luke 24, verses 50 to 51) and at the beginning of Acts (chapter 1, verses 9 to 11). By doing this, Luke underlines that Jesus is the reigning Lord of the church. The fourfold repetition of the phrase 'into heaven' (Acts 1, verses 10 and 11) emphasises his exalted status and present domain. The message to be proclaimed by the apostles is that Jesus whom you Jews crucified is now enthroned in heaven. He has ascended to sit on the throne as the Davidic Messiah and been designated 'Lord' (Acts 2, verse 36).

The final departure of Jesus anticipates the giving of the Holy Spirit and allows for the challenge to the apostles to be given once more. The angelic figures who appear as Jesus ascends tell the disciples not to stand gazing up into heaven in wonder, but to get on with the task. As they have seen Jesus go into heaven, so in like manner he will return.

The mission is urgent because it is set in the interim between the ascension of Jesus and his final return. This passage thus corresponds with Jesus' own statement in Mark 13, verse 10 that the gospel must be preached to all nations before the end can come.

In Luke's account of the ascension, he brings us

face-to-face with two difficult-to-comprehend Christian truths. The first is, that Jesus visibly ascended into heaven after forty days of resurrection appearances. There was a moment of time when Jesus physically entered the world and a moment of time when he physically departed.

And the second truth is that, just as Jesus departed, he will return. There will be a second coming of Christ. We are forbidden to speculate on when this will be but, when Jesus returns, it will be sudden and visible. We are to be ready.

Waiting on God (verses 12 to 14)

Between the fortieth day 'on which Jesus ascended' and the gift of the Holy Spirit at the feast of Pentecost — the feast on the fiftieth day after Passover — there was a ten-day waiting period in Luke's chronological scheme. In this little scene, Luke has the disciples waiting in prayer for God to act. In verse 13 he gives a list of the eleven faithful apostles who are said to be with the women,[2] and Mary the mother of Jesus and his brothers (verse 14). In introducing the next story, Luke says the number of persons was about 120.

Luke's mention of the women, Mary and the brothers of Jesus is not surprising. Luke has the greatest interest in and the most positive attitude towards women of all the New Testament writers and he consistently describes Jesus' family as true believers (see Luke 8, verses 19 to 21). James the brother of Jesus eventually becomes the leader of the Jerusalem church (Acts 12, verse 17; chapter 15, verse 13; and chapter 21, verse 18).

The reference to prayer is also characteristically Lucan. In Luke-Acts, there are more comments about prayer than in any other part of the New Testament.[3] Luke usually has Jesus or other key characters praying immediately before some important event or act of God.

The prayers of these believers, Luke points out, were *united* and *persevering*. The RSV speaks of them praying 'with one accord' (verse 14). The same Greek term translated by these words is used again of the united prayer of the early Christians in Acts 4, verse 24 and of a united decision in Acts 15, verse 25. The thought recalls Jesus' promise that 'if two of you *agree* about anything you ask, it will be done for you by my Father in heaven. For where two or three are gathered in my name, I am there among them' (Matthew 18, verses 19 and 20).

The word translated by the RSV as 'devoted' (verse 14) means to be busy or persistent (see Acts 2, verse 42; and Acts 6, verse 4). The disciples persevered in prayer as they waited for Jesus' promise to be fulfilled (Acts 1, verses 4, 5 and 8).

Replacement of Judas (verses 15 to 26)

With the apostasy and death of Judas, a twelfth apostle was seen to be needed. The full complement of twelve apostles is important to Luke. The number was of special typological significance. Just as there had been twelve patriarchs as the nucleus and founding fathers of historic Israel, so there were to be twelve apostles as the nucleus and founding fathers of the restored Israel, called into being by the Messiah.

Luke is not interested in what each of the twelve did; he is interested only in the fact that there were twelve apostles to establish the Christian community. In Luke's understanding, the special role of the twelve is *to bear witness* to the life, teaching, death and resurrection of Jesus. In their role as the founding fathers of the restored Israel, they are the bridge between Jesus and the new Christian community: the guarantors of the gospel message.

Peter provided leadership for the first Christians in the early days and was involved in some missionary work (chapters 10 and 11), but the special and unique role for Peter and the other apostles was *to bear witness* to Jesus' ministry and resurrection.[4] The terminology used is drawn from the Jewish law courts. A witness is one who guarantees the facts. As Jewish law normally excluded women from bearing witness, Luke could hardly have included women in this select group. The main reason, however, that women were not included amongst the twelve is that only twelve men could be the typological counterpart of the twelve patriarchs.

The oft-heard argument that women cannot be Christian priests/pastors because the twelve were all men does not hold water. The twelve were not congregational leaders, they had no successors (eyewitnesses cannot be replaced) and, when the number of apostles was enlarged after the church was firmly established to include such people as Paul and Barnabas and many others (the so-called missionary apostles), we find reference to at least one woman apostle, Junia (Romans 16, verse 7).

Luke goes on to say that Peter saw the need to replace Judas as being foretold in the Old Testament. He quotes Psalm 69, verse 25 and Psalm 109, verse 8. The account of Judas' death is described somewhat differently in Matthew 27, verses 3 to 10, but the stories can be reconciled. The three qualifications needed for candidature are:

(a) to be a man;
(b) to have accompanied Jesus throughout his ministry, and
(c) to be a witness of his resurrection (verse 22).

Two men were put forward: Joseph, called Barsabbas, and Matthias. After prayer, they cast lots and Matthias was chosen. The casting of lots in this instance draws on the Old Testament belief that God can use such a method to reveal his will (see Proverbs 16, verse 37). The point is that the choice between these two equal candidates was ultimately made by God. Matthias was God's choice.

Discussion questions

Talking it through

1 Luke reminds his patron that his second book naturally flows out of his first (Acts 1, verses 1 and 2)
Why does Luke seek to link his Gospel and Acts so tightly? Is it just a historical connection?

2 Explain why the disciples' question in verse 6 showed that at this stage they did not understand Jesus' mission. What were they thinking?

3 Is the angels' advice (verse 11) meant to indicate to us that:
   (a) we should not waste time meditating and reflecting
   (b) we should forget about normal employment and get on with preaching
   (c) we are to relax and let God work his purposes out
   (d) something else?

4 Are verses 12 to 14 just the natural response to fear and persecution? Are the early disciples a positive role model? Was there a relationship between their praying and what happened afterwards in chapter 2?

5 The disciples were hardly squeamish about the failure of Judas (verses 15 to 20). Was God judging Judas? Does God judge people in this way today?

6 What do you think is the significance of appointing a *twelfth* apostle? In what way is this preparation for establishing the Christian community?

34/Preparation for the community

Widening our horizons

1 Why does Jesus answer the disciples the way he does (verse 7)? Were they exceeding their responsibility? How can we be similarly guilty? Compare such contemporary 'burning issues' as:
(a) the state of the Middle East
(b) environmental degradation
(c) the possibility of a nuclear holocaust.

2 Jesus went *up* and *sits at God's right hand*. Has heaven a geographic location and material reality? How do you understand the whereabouts and the character of heaven? Do you find this:
(a) frightening
(b) confusing
(c) mind-extending
(d) fascinating?
Why?

3 Think of contemporary attempts to try old men for war crimes long since past, or to put corporate criminals behind bars. To what extent can we expect God to vindicate his name or reputation by punishing wrongdoers *in their lifetime?* Does he?

4 Is it right to say that the decision made in verses 23 to 26 was peculiar to first century Jewish culture? What would first century observers make of our acceptance of the following:
  (a) putting parents in old people's homes
  (b) demanding equal opportunity in the workplace
  (c) advertising church positions in the press?

5 What is prayer? Using verses 12 to 14 as a starting point, indicate what prayer might mean to:
  (a) a Christian
  (b) a Buddhist
  (c) a Muslim
  (d) a non-religious person who is desperate?

2
The founding of the community

ACTS CHAPTER 2

PENTECOSTAL CHURCHES ARE THOSE which have broken away from the mainline, older denominations and formed new groupings with such names as 'The Assemblies of God', 'The Apostolic Church' and 'The Christian Revival Crusade'. They take their generic name from the Jewish feast of Pentecost, the day on which the Holy Spirit, the third member of the Trinity, came upon the Christian community.

In all Pentecostal churches, the person and work of the Holy Spirit is given great prominence. They maintain that in the older churches, tradition and one-man ministry has so often quenched the Spirit. Their vitality of faith and commitment to evangelism have made them the fastest growing segment of the church. They hold to the orthodox faith, and their emphasis on all Christians having a part to play is a biblical truth that needs to be learnt by others. Their exuberant worship is a personal preference, not a matter of doctrine.

They differ from most others, however, in their interpretation of some stories in the book of Acts, from which they argue that every Christian needs a post-conversion experience called 'the baptism in the Holy Spirit' which is usually evidenced by tongue-speaking.

In this chapter and later, this claim will be considered. We need to ask ourselves, as we get to grips with the text itself, whether or not this interpretation is what Luke is teaching.

The writer's agenda

This chapter is the most important in Luke's second volume. It introduces the major practical and theological issues about which he is writing. The pattern is similar to that in Luke's Gospel. There, the birth narratives prepare for the coming of the Holy Spirit upon Jesus at his baptism (Luke 3, verses 21 and 22), marking the commencement of the Messianic ministry. This is followed by Jesus' first sermon given in the synagogue at Nazareth (chapter 4, verses 16 to 30) which introduces most of the main themes Luke will develop in his Gospel.

In the same way, Acts 1 prepares for the coming

of the Holy Spirit on the first disciples on the day of Pentecost. This is followed by Peter's first sermon which, like the one at Nazareth, introduces most of the main themes Luke will develop in Acts. It seems Luke is subtly saying that the messianic ministry, begun when Jesus was endowed with the Holy Spirit, is continued by the Spirit-filled disciples after Pentecost.

The day of Pentecost (verses 1 to 13)
The word 'Pentecost' is a transliteration of the Greek word meaning 'fiftieth'. It was the name given to the Jewish feast which came fifty days after the Passover when the angel of death passed over the houses of all those residing in Egypt in slavery under Pharoah, the event that precipitated the Jews' release. Originally it was a harvest festival,[1] but by the time of Jesus the Jews had come to associate the giving of the Law to Moses at Mt Sinai with the day of Pentecost.

Just as the old agreement or covenant began with the giving of the Law at the feast of Pentecost, so the beginning of the new covenant is marked by the giving of the Holy Spirit. The first epoch was an epoch characterised by law; the second epoch is an epoch characterised by the Holy Spirit.

The advent of the Spirit is described in terms of an Old Testament appearance of God, a 'theophany'. The house in which the disciples were waiting was suddenly filled with a sound *like* the rush of a mighty wind' (verse 2). The wind symbolised God's presence. The second symbol was fire — another feature of Old Testament theophanies, especially the one at Sinai when the Law was first given (Exodus 19, verse 18). Then we are told, 'All of them were filled with the Holy Spirit and began to speak in other languages as the Spirit gave them ability' (verse 4).

Luke speaks of people being 'filled with the Spirit' when they are initially endowed from on high, as is the case here (see Acts 9, verse 17), and also when Christians are given a special measure of the Spirit to equip them for a particular ministry of limited duration.[2] In other words, Luke allows that a 'Spirit-filled' person can also be given a special filling for some distinct task. This means that to be filled with the Spirit does not exclude the possibility of future fillings of the Spirit.

It should be noted, too, that to be filled with the Spirit is but one way Luke describes the coming of the Spirit upon a person. When he speaks of the Spirit being 'poured out' on someone (Acts 2, verse 17; and Acts 10, verse 45), of people 'receiving the Spirit' (Acts 10, verse 47), or of them being 'baptised with the Holy Spirit' (Acts 1, verse 5; and Acts 11, verse 16), the same phenomenon is in mind. In Luke's understanding, the one basic characteristic of a Christian is the presence of the Holy Spirit. A disciple of Christ is one in whom the Spirit dwells.

Luke suggests that the normal pattern is for a

person to repent and believe, be baptised in water and at that point receive the Holy Spirit (Acts 2, verse 38), but he allows that in the early days of the Christian mission some strange things happened. God did not always act according to a set pattern (he still doesn't!). The Samaritans believed in Christ and only later received the Spirit (Acts 8, verses 4 to 24). In another case, the Spirit was given before people were baptised (Acts 10, verses 44 to 47) and some followers of John the Baptist, who had been baptised in water, were given the Spirit later when Paul instructed them more fully (Acts 19, verses 1 to 6).

When Luke says the Spirit-filled disciples spoke 'in other tongues' (verse 4), he means they spoke in different languages. In verses 7 and 8, he makes this point explicitly. This tongue-speaking may be therefore *contrasted* with the tongue-speaking discussed just once in the Pauline epistles in 1 Corinthians 12 to 14 where interpretation is needed.

The point is that the events on the day of Pentecost were unique. This was the *first* giving of the Spirit; this was the inauguration of the age of the Holy Spirit. The background of thought is that the gift of the Spirit overcomes the divisions among people caused by sin, spoken about in the story of the tower of Babel (Genesis 9, verses 1 to 9). The Jews 'from every nation under heaven' (verse 5), who all spoke different languages, symbolise divided humanity. The fact that they all heard of 'the mighty works of God' (verse 11, RSV or 'God's deeds of power', NRSV) in their own speech foreshadows the mission to the whole world.

Peter's first sermon (verses 14 to 41)
This is the first of some twenty-four sermons in Acts. They take up about a quarter of the book. Some are given with a degree of fullness, others in brief form, but all of them are to be seen as summaries. They are included as part of the overall structure of Acts and are both medium and message. Although addressed to a particular audience in the past, they are in direct speech and so, whenever read, the sermons once more speak.

❏ *The strange phenomena explained (verses 14 to 21)*

The strange behaviour of the recipients of the Spirit raises a number of questions in the minds of those present (verses 12 and 13). Peter stands up to explain the significance of these events and then moves into an evangelistic sermon addressed to Jews. He says these men are not drunk with wine, but filled with the Spirit. This has happened as fulfilment of the prophecy of Joel (Joel 2, verses 28 to 32).

The giving of the Spirit is a sign that 'the last days', literally the 'eschatological days', have dawned. The prophet predicted that, when God visited his people, he would pour out his Spirit on young and old, men and women and that they would prophesy. In this context, prophesying means to proclaim the mighty acts of God in the power of the Spirit.

This ministry, it should be noted, is given to both sexes! The Spirit is for equal opportunity for men and women. Luke never mentions the subordination of women and, wherever possible, places men and women side by side as equals in the Jesus community. The 'wonders in the heavens above and signs on the earth beneath' (verse 19, NIV), spoken of by the prophet Joel, are probably thought of as fulfilled when the disciples spoke in other languages on earth and Jesus was raised on high to heaven.

❏ *Jesus' death and resurrection explained (verses 22 to 36)*

Peter now introduces Jesus of Nazareth whom he says was crucified by lawless men (verses 22 to 33). He then speaks of his resurrection and exaltation, the matters of most importance to him.

A number of quotes from the Old Testament are used to show that this was anticipated and to explain the significance of the resurrection and exaltation. First, appeal is made to Psalm 16, verses 8 to 11 (to be found in Acts 2, verses 22 to 28). Peter suggests that as these words could not have applied to David himself, they must point to the coming Messiah (verses 29 to 31).

Then second, Psalm 110, verse 1 is quoted to

support the claim that Jesus now reigns in heaven (verses 33 to 35). The grand climax is reached when Peter declares that this Jesus whom they crucified has been made by God both Lord and Christ (verse 36). The blame for the crucifixion is laid at the feet of the Jews of that day.

❏ *The hearers' response*
  (verses 37 to 41)
This bold proclamation caused the crowd to cry out, 'What shall we do?' Peter's reply was that they must repent, be baptised and receive the Holy Spirit (verse 38). Luke says that about three thousand people responded. The first Christian sermon had startling results.

The lifestyle of the earliest community (verses 42 to 47)

A brief description of the life of the first Spirit-filled Christians follows.

In verse 42, Luke lists four activities in which these early believers engrossed themselves. It could be thought that the list simply mentions four separate things important to the first believers — elements which were common features when the Christians gathered together.

As the special recipients of Jesus' teaching, it was natural that the apostles were the first teachers in the Christian community. They passed on what

Jesus himself had taught them. Apparently, their teaching was so effective that soon others also became teachers, for we hear very little elsewhere in Acts of the teaching role of the twelve. They are more characteristically drawn as evangelists.

In Greek, the word translated 'fellowship' conveys the idea of 'sharing' someone or something, rather than a warm feeling of intimacy which is suggested by the English word. The fellowship the first believers enjoyed was a sharing in the life of Christ and with each other. It was something they held in common. The breaking of bread alludes to a meal-setting for the celebration of the Lord's supper (see 1 Corinthians 11, verses 20 to 29). The prayers are almost certainly communal prayers. The synagogue was often called 'a house of prayer', for communal prayer was an essential feature of Jewish worship.

In verses 43 to 47, Luke gives one of his summaries to conclude a section in his story. As the sharing of possessions is discussed more fully later (in Acts 4, verses 32 to 37), we need not consider this matter just now. At this point we simply note that the sharing of goods mentioned in verses 44 to 45 was a *voluntary* expression of spiritual vitality and faith.

In speaking of 'fear' (verse 43), Luke means that unbelievers showed some 'awe' (NIV, NRSV) when they heard about and saw the wonders and signs performed by the apostles. Apparently, this did not always lead to belief. The fear of God did not lead to faith in God.

These early believers did not immediately break with other Jews or withdraw from the temple (verse 46). At first, the early Christians saw themselves as loyal Jews who stood apart solely because they had recognised that Jesus was the Messiah and had been endowed with the Spirit. Thus they continued to meet in the temple, but supplemented this with house-meetings. The early Christians' spiritual vitality was contagious: 'The Lord added to their number day by day those who were being saved'(verse 4).

Concluding thoughts on tongues

In answer to the question as to whether or not all Christians should speak in tongues, Acts 2 seems to suggest the answer is 'No'.

Luke describes a once-only, unique event — the first giving of the Holy Spirit. The tongue-speaking on that occasion was quite miraculous. People of many different nationalities *each* heard the apostles praising God in their own language without an interpreter. Associated with the tongues were flames on each disciple's head, the noise of a mighty rushing wind and the shaking of the house. Should not these signs also be expected if we were all supposed to speak in a foreign language when we first received the Spirit?

Paul's discussion of tongues alludes to a quite different phenomenon. For him, tongue-speaking is but *one* of many spiritual gifts — a gift not given to all Christians (1 Corinthians 12, verses 7 to 31). This gift is a more mundane speaking than seen at Pentecost, for an interpretation is always needed. Paul only mentions tongue-speaking when writing to the Corinthians. We don't know if any other early church knew or encouraged this particular gift.

Discussion questions

Talking it through

1 Why is it particularly appropriate that the Holy Spirit came during the festival of *Pentecost*? What was being celebrated?

2 What is particularly powerful about the term 'filled with the Spirit'? Who is this Spirit? What idea does the word 'filled' conjure up?

3 Compare 'speaking in tongues' on the day of Pentecost and the phenomenon known as 'speaking in tongues' in some present-day churches? In what ways are they the same? In what ways are they different?

4 'Christianity is down-to-earth.' What is there in this chapter of Acts that supports this statement?

Widening our horizons

1 How is God's power demonstrated by each of the following:
  (a) the events of the day of Pentecost
  (b) the survival of the Christian church in its first two centuries of persecution
  (c) the faithfulness of remnants of the church in Hitler's Germany or Communist China?
  Is there a link between these events?

2 Imagine yourself at the original day of Pentecost. How does it compare with an event of great pageantry that you have witnessed — a coronation, for example? At what points does the comparison break down? Why?

3 Each of the following powerful speeches was addressing an important question in people's minds. In each case, what was the question?
  (a) Winston Churchill's speeches in World War II
  (b) Abraham Lincoln's speech at Gettysburg in 1863

(c) Martin Luther's speech at Worms in 1521
(d) Peter's speech at Pentecost

Having this as a basis, what gives these speeches power? Can this teach us anything about when we should speak and when we should be silent?

4 At what points are each of the following people true descendants of these early Christians:
 (a) the Italian aristocrat of the Middle Ages who entered a monastery
 (b) the brilliant graduate of a Western university who returns to his Third World country as an evangelist
 (c) the unimpaired person who lives in a community for the mentally handicapped as an equal
 (d) a Christian community sharing a common purse?

3
Membership of the community

ACTS CHAPTER 3

IN RECENT YEARS, MOST CHRISTIANS have regained an interest in the healing ministry. They have come to see that Christian faith must impinge on all of life. We are not simply called on to repent and believe, but also to know the refreshing touch of God's presence which should change every part of our life (see chapter 3, verse 19).

In our parish church, we periodically invite people to come forward for prayer and the laying-on of hands and we have seen wonderful answers to prayer. The whole church remains in prayer as people kneel at the communion rails and a group prays for whatever need is expressed. Usually people ask for God's help with everyday problems — marriages under stress; wayward children; an impending visit to hospital; an aching back.

Once a woman brought her husband who was dying of cancer to our church service. We prayed for God to meet him in his need, but a week or so later he died. I visited the bereaved wife expecting her to be very disappointed and perhaps sceptical. Instead, she was exuberant. She said there had been a wonderful healing. They had come home from church and for the first time in his life her husband wanted to pray and read the Bible. They had spent an exhilarating week together in the presence of God. She was confident he had now gone to heaven.

At our church, prayer has been answered, but we have not seen blind eyes opened, withered legs restored or the dead raised. These are the sorts of miracles mentioned in the Gospels and Acts. Should these totally miraculous events still be expected today? Some Christians say 'Yes'; others 'No'. Most of us are not quite sure. What should we believe?

The healing of the lame man (verses 1 to 10)

The story opens with Peter and John entering the temple at 3.00 p.m. to join in communal prayers with other Jews (the Jewish day began at 6.00 a.m.; it was the ninth hour after that). A lame man, crippled from birth, asks them for a gift.

Luke emphasises the reality of his incapacities.

He has been unable to walk all his life and, at the time, he is somewhat over forty years old (chapter 4, verse 22). Peter commands him to look at them and then, in the name of Jesus of Nazareth, commands him to walk (verse 6). He raises him up and the man is able to leap and walk. This is no healing of an ache in the back or a pain in the knee. It is a powerful act of God, an example of 'the wonders and signs' (chapter 2, verse 43) seen amongst the earliest Christians.

There is a story that once that great medieval theologian Thomas Aquinas visited the Pope. The pontiff showed Thomas the glories of the Vatican — the great buildings, the works of art and other treasures. He said, 'Thomas, no longer need Peter say, "Silver and gold have I none".' 'Yes, Holy Father,' said the wise old theologian, 'but no longer can Peter say, "In the name of Jesus Christ of Nazareth, walk."'

When Peter heals in 'the name of Jesus Christ' (chapter 3, verse 6), it means he acts with the authority of Jesus. Jesus healed in his own power; Peter can only heal or preach in the power mediated through him by the risen Lord of the church (see chapter 3, verse 12).

The sermon following the miracle (verses 11 to 26)

As was the case on the day of Pentecost, the miracle

gathers a crowd and some explanation is needed. Again, Peter takes the opportunity to proclaim Christ.

The apostle first disclaims that the miracle was due to his or John's power or piety; he then goes on to proclaim Christ as the suffering servant foretold in the book of Isaiah (see Isaiah 52, verse 13 to chapter 53, verse 12).

Note the titles given to Jesus: 'God's servant' (chapter 3, verses 13 and 26), 'the holy and righteous one' (verse 14), and 'the author of life' (verse 15). The point Peter underlines is that the Jesus who suffered and died is the one God raised from the dead (verse 15) and glorified (verses 13 and 21). This all happened, says Peter, as prophesied (verse 18). If fellow Jews had known the scriptures better, Peter argues, they would not have 'acted in ignorance' (verse 17) and crucified Christ.

In verse 22, Peter adds yet another title for Jesus. He equates him with 'the prophet' whom Moses predicted would come in the last days (see Deuteronomy 18, verses 15 and 16). This prophet, Moses said, you Jews should 'listen to' —that is, obey (verse 22). Jesus is not simply one of the prophets; he is *the* prophet.

What really stands out is the Christ-centredness of Peter's sermon and its dependence on the Old Testament. He points the crowd's attention away from the healed cripple and the apostles and directs it to Jesus, the crucified Messiah, or Christ. Peter insists that if the Jewish leaders had really known the Old Testament, they would have seen that it identified Jesus of Nazareth as the prophetic hope. They acted against him out of ignorance (verse 17).

There is now only one appropriate response, says Peter. They must *repent* (verse 19). Repentance is one of Luke's favourite terms. He uses the noun or the verb more than any other New Testament writer. The meaning of repent is clarified by the addition of the words 'and turn to God' (GNB — the RSV translation 'turn again' is mistaken). Repentance involves changing one's mind or changing direction. It is an about-turn.

Three blessings are promised to Peter's audience if they repent:

* *First*, their sins will be 'blotted out' (verse 19b). The Greek term means to wash off, erase or obliterate. Ancient writing on papyrus did not hold like modern ink on paper. To erase writing, a wipe with a wet cloth was all that was needed. So when men or women repent, God wipes away past sins and leaves the slate clean.
* *Second*, 'times of refreshing' will come (verse 19c). God forgives our past sins and in the present brings refreshment. Into life he bestows something new. Elsewhere in Acts this present refreshment is identified with the Holy Spirit.
* *Third*, Peter promises the return of Christ (verse 20). In the present Jesus reigns in heaven (verse 21), but there will come a day when he returns

to establish the universal reign of God. The present is the interim age when repentance is possible.

In this sermon, Peter not only clarifies the status of Jesus, but also the status of those who repent or do not repent. Peter says that those who do not repent 'shall be destroyed from the people' (verse 23).

The Greek word *laos*, translated 'people', is a technical term which means 'the people of God', the Jews. So what Peter is saying is, if you Jews don't repent, you will cease to be God's people. In Jesus, God is sifting the Jewish nation. He is calling out true Israel. The people of God are those who recognise that Jesus of Nazareth is the crucified and exalted Messiah. Unbelieving Jews are to be cut out of their inheritance and believing Gentiles are to be included in that inheritance.

We thus see here how Luke defines the church (understood as the people of God — see Acts 20, verse 28). It is renewed or restored Israel. The Christian community has its foundation in Judaism, but the gospel makes membership of the people of God dependent not on race, but on a recognition of Jesus as both Lord and Christ (chapter 2, verse 36).

Wonders and signs

In the book of Acts, the gospel triumphs as God achieves his purposes in and through his servants.

God's presence is never far away as far as Luke is concerned. It is therefore not really possible to separate the miraculous from the non-miraculous in Luke's story.

Nevertheless, Luke does single out a number of particularly dramatic acts of God to underline that the God revealed in Jesus Christ is all-powerful and willing to act on behalf of his people. These special demonstrations of power Luke usually calls 'wonders and signs'.[1]

He can, however, and often does, mention such demonstrations of power without using this terminology.[2] These miracles, Professor Lampe says, 'are an integral part of the apostolic witness as Luke understands it, and they are characteristic signs of the new age which the ascension has inaugurated'. He also notes that Luke invariably associates these demonstrations of God's power with the preaching of the gospel.

This is clearly seen in this chapter. Peter and John heal the lame man and then proceed to proclaim Jesus Christ as the crucified Messiah.

Healing

In the face of claim and counter-claim about healing in the church today, a balanced, fully biblical answer is needed.

We must reject completely the idea that miracles are no longer possible. The God of the Bible remains the same. He is all-powerful and nothing is beyond him. The danger of our secular, materialistic age is that our vision of God may be too small. On the other hand, the suggestion that God *always* wants to heal physical ills must also be rejected. The Bible does not teach this.

The book of Job is given to refute the idea that believing, good-living people will not suffer personal tragedy or illness. Job is described as 'blameless and upright, one who feared God and turned away from evil' (Job 1, verse 1). Nevertheless God allowed Satan to destroy his family, take his wealth and afflict him with a terrible physical illness (chapter 1, verse 11 onwards). Job's prayers for deliverance were not answered. It was God's will to allow all this to happen, we are told.

Likewise in the New Testament, Paul suffered from some painful ongoing physical malady and, although he prayed three times to God for relief, the reply was, 'My grace is sufficient for you, for my power is made perfect in weakness' (2 Corinthians 12, verse 9). Then there is Timothy, Paul's most faithful fellow labourer. The apostle speaks of his frequent illnesses (1 Timothy 5, verse 23). Finally, we mention Trophimus whom Paul had to leave ill at Miletus (2 Timothy 4, verse 20). It must not have been God's will to heal him at that time.

This biblical teaching is confirmed by the experience of Christian living. Some of the finest, most faithful Christian people have suffered a great deal from physical illness, despite their prayers for relief, and some have died young. A classic example is David Watson. He was a most Christlike man, gracious and prayerful and a wonderful evangelist. But at the age of fifty, he developed cancer and, despite the prayers of countless people who believed in healing, he died. It was God's will to take him. Someone has said that you cannot have a biblical view of healing unless you also have a biblical view of suffering. The Bible nowhere suggests that God wills always to heal or to prolong life.

All our prayers, therefore, are an attempt to come into harmony with the will of God. Sometimes he wills to heal miraculously; often he wills to be glorified through our suffering and he gives us the grace to stand and to grow through it. There is no promise in the Bible that faith will shield us from suffering or lead to our quick recovery if we get sick. The scriptures, in fact, teach quite clearly that following Christ involves taking up the cross and suffering in many ways.[3]

When we are sick, or friends or loved ones are sick, we should always pray for God to show mercy. He always answers such prayers. Now and then the sickness completely vanishes. Miraculous healing occurs. At other times, he answers by giving us strength to endure, or a completely new attitude to our health problems. Christians also call this healing and thank God for it.

Seeking the prayer of others, especially the leaders of our Christian family, is recommended by James

(James 5, verse 14). Prayer, however, is not an alternative to medical assistance. When sick, we should pray *and* seek the best medical help available. Modern medicine is one of God's good gifts to humankind. Sometimes God heals without medical assistance, but usually he heals through the aid of medicine.

The various kinds of God-given healing may be distinguished nevertheless. There is healing which comes as the body heals itself, often with the aid of surgery or medicine. Here we remember that doctors do not heal; they assist the healing process.

Then there is the healing of wrong attitudes, especially in our relationship with God. This comes as God helps us to see our suffering in a new light or gives us added strength to face it. In such instances the word 'healing' is used to mean 'wholeness'. It is really a healing of the human spirit by the Holy Spirit.

Then third, there is miraculous healing as illustrated by the healing of the lame man by Peter and John. Such physical healing has always been very rare. Luke emphasises the lame man's lifelong disabilities. He had been a cripple since birth. His muscles would have been withered and his joints partly fused. The healing took place completely and instantaneously, as Peter and John gave the command (not even the laying-on of hands, prayer or anointing with oil is mentioned). He stood up, walked and leaped in the air. Not only were believers convinced that this man had been miraculously cured, but so also were unbelievers (Acts 3, verse 10; Acts 4, verses 14 and 16).

As we said at the beginning, there is no reason why God cannot still act in this way today but, once we define such healings as 'miraculous', then we are saying we don't expect God to act like this every day. A miracle is by definition something quite exceptional, a deviation from the norm. The sovereign Lord who is master of the whole universe does not usually act in this way.

If he allows us to be hurt in an accident, or contract some disease, he normally allows matters to follow their normal course and expects us to use the medical knowledge and drugs which are also his gifts to humankind.

If he always healed miraculously when we prayed in faith, we would not know the phenomenon of a miracle. It would be how God usually acted — a mundane event for Christians.

So then to sum up:

* God can act miraculously and sometimes still does, but this is not the usual or normal way he acts, especially today in developed countries where he has provided excellent health care.
* God can allow faithful and devout Christians such as Paul to suffer and even to die young. His power can be made perfect in weakness.
* God usually answers prayers for relief from suf-

fering by providing a strength hitherto unknown — a healing of the human spirit by the divine Spirit.
* In every situation, we are commanded to pray. God delights in the prayers of his people and this is how we find the perfect will of God for ourselves.

Discussion questions

Talking it through

1 What is the difference between Jesus' and Peter's healings? What *added* element does the Thomas Aquinas story contain?

2 What sorts of feelings would have gone through your mind if you had heard Peter's sermon? As a Jew, what would have been particularly difficult?

3 What does the statement on healing (pages 56 to 61) teach us about prayer? Does prayer have any point?

4 What is the basis of membership of the Christian community?

Widening our horizons

1 What constitutes a miracle? Would you class the following as miracles:
  (a) a person wanting to act in God's interest rather than his own
  (b) one house remaining standing when a devastating bushfire destroys all others
  (c) pulling a rabbit out of a hat?

2 'Peter's sermon is necessary to explain the healing.' Is it? How would you explain, if you had to, each of the following:
  (a) a particularly kind deed you felt compelled to do
  (b) a particularly evil deed you felt compelled to do
  (c) your observation of a breathtaking panoramic view?
  Do you see such interpretations of happenings as important?

3 What elements of repentance as described in the New Testament are present in each of the following life situations?

(a) You are forced by the evidence to acknowledge that you had destroyed an innocent person's reputation without knowing the facts.
(b) You have a low opinion of a well-known public figure until you meet him and are charmed out of your socks.
(c) You have placed great faith in a supposed friend and then are given irrefutable evidence, against everything you believe, that this faith was unjustified?

4 What words of comfort would you provide for each of the following:
(a) the wife of a person with malignant cancer
(b) the daughter of a person of faith martyred for his religious principles
(c) the father of a child dying of leukemia?

4
Signs of trouble in the community

ACTS CHAPTER 4

THE OPENING CHAPTERS OF ACTS paint a very positive picture. The disciples obediently wait in Jerusalem, persevering in prayer, and then the Holy Spirit is poured out. Peter preaches in power and about 3 000 believe. There seems to be an openness to the gospel by the Jews and their leaders.

When Peter and John as good, law-abiding Jews go to the temple as is their custom, they are asked for help by a lame man. In the name of Jesus, he is miraculously healed and again Peter has the opportunity to preach to a crowd. Having reached the end of Acts 3, we might think the progress of the gospel was to be one triumphant march forward as people of goodwill gladly accepted the good news about Jesus Christ. The events of Acts 4 quickly dispel this idea.

Opposition to the gospel and persecution of its heralds are introduced. The Jewish leaders rise up in anger as they perceive that the ancestral faith of Judaism is under threat. If the Holy Spirit is the chief actor of the first three chapters of Acts, then the chief actor in the next three chapters is Satan.

Working through the Jewish leaders (chapter 4, verses 13 to 22), in members of the church (Ananias and Sapphira, chapter 5, verses 1 to 6), and through divisions amongst the believers (chapter 6, verses 1 to 6), Satan is seen to be very active. In a way, Luke is giving the same warning as made by Peter, only he makes his point by recounting history. Peter writes: 'Discipline yourselves, keep alert. Like a roaring lion your adversary the devil prowls around, looking for someone to devour.' (1 Peter 5, verse 8).

Acts 4 divides into two quite distinct sections. Verses 1 to 31 tell of what happens after Peter and John heal the blind man in the temple; verses 32 to 37 describe the quality of the communal life enjoyed by the first disciples.

The healing of the lame man made a great impression on the ordinary people, but it aroused the opposition of the Jewish leaders. In verses 1 to 31, four successive developments are mentioned: the arrest of Peter and John and their overnight imprisonment (verses 1 to 4); the hearing before the

Sanhedrin at which Peter offers his defence (verses 5 to 12); and the prayer of the church in response to the apostles' release (verses 23 to 31).

The arrest of Peter and John
(verses 1 to 4)
While Peter and John were still speaking, a group of leading Jews, members of the Sanhedrin, the supreme governing council of the Jews, came and arrested the two apostles. They were annoyed by the apostles' message, Luke tells us, because they were 'proclaiming in Jesus the resurrection from the dead'. The Sadducees who controlled the Sanhedrin were opponents of the idea of a resurrection (see Luke 20, verses 27 to 40 and Acts 23, verses 6 to 8).

As it was late in the day, no trial could take place. For safe keeping the apostles were put in prison. Luke points out that this dramatic ending to the apostles' sermon in no way lessened its impact. Many believed so that the number of Christians increased to about 5 000.

The trial and defence of Peter and John
(verses 5 to 12)
The next day, the Sanhedrin assembled and John and Peter were put on trial. Luke mentions some of the important people present in verses 5 and 6. The question put to the apostles does not concern the resurrection, but the miracle. The Jewish rulers

asked, 'By what power or by what name did you do this?'

Jesus' promise that he would help his disciples when on trial (see Luke 12, verse 11 onwards; Luke 21, verse 14 onwards) was fulfilled as Peter was given a special infilling of the Spirit to equip him in this situation (verse 8). He boldly stated that the miracle was performed 'by the name of Jesus Christ of Nazareth, whom you crucified, whom God raised from the dead' (verse 10). Alluding to Psalm 118, verse 22, Peter spoke of Jesus as the rejected stone who has now become the cornerstone.

In speaking of the healing (verse 9), Luke uses the word 'sozo', which also means salvation. He again uses this word in verse 12 where a wider healing — salvation — was offered to the Jewish rulers. Luke insists that only in the name of Jesus can salvation be found.

The Sanhedrin's decision (verses 13 to 22)

What struck the Jewish leaders most forcibly was the boldness of Peter and John. This they saw as surprising because they perceived that the apostles were not instructed in the Law.

This is what Luke means when he says the Jewish leaders judged Peter and John to be 'uneducated and ordinary men'. The only way the Jewish leaders could explain their boldness and eloquence was the influence of Jesus: 'They recognised that they had been with Jesus' (verse 13).

When H.M. Stanley discovered David Livingstone in Central Africa, he lived with him for some months. Later he wrote: 'If I had been with him any longer, I would have been compelled to become a Christian and he never spoke to me about it at all.'

Livingstone had not spent time with the historical Jesus like Peter and John, but Stanley perceived that the great missionary doctor 'had been with Jesus'. He was different — his faith transformed his life.

The presence of the man who had been healed (verse 14) and the lack of other charges gave the Sanhedrin few options. In private discussion, they decided the most important thing was to stop the story of the miracle circulating. They therefore decided to forbid the apostles to speak or teach in the name of Jesus (verses 12 to 18). However, Peter and John refused, saying, 'we cannot keep from speaking about what we have seen and heard' (verse 20). The Jewish leaders warned them once more and then released them.

The prayer of praise (verses 23 to 31)

When Peter and John were reunited with their Christian friends, a prayer of praise and thanksgiving was offered to God by the assembled community. In the opening ascription, God is addressed as 'Sovereign Lord' (verse 24). This testifies to a faith in an all-powerful God who is able to save and defend his people, a God who hears and answers prayers.

The prayer then draws on Psalm 2 where the raging of ungodly Gentile rulers is seen to be powerless against 'the Lord's anointed' ('the anointed one' means in Hebrew the 'Messiah', or in Greek the 'Christ').

Jesus is, of course, the one anointed by the Spirit in a unique way (see Luke 3, verses 21 and 22). In Acts 4, verse 27, the Gentile rulers, foreshadowed in the Psalm, are equated with Herod and Pontius Pilate.

The petitionary section of the prayer asks not for safety or security, but rather that God's servants might speak the word with 'boldness' (verse 29, see verse 13) as God works 'signs and wonders. . . through the name of your holy servant Jesus' (verse 30). Again we see a connection between preaching and accompanying miracles.

The effect of the prayer was remarkable (verse 31). The place in which they were gathered shook as if an earthquake had occurred. Here again is a 'theophany', an appearance of God.[1] This symbolised God had heard their prayer, but the boldness of the disciples in having the words necessary, the very matter they had asked for, equally demonstrates God's answer.

This boldness is again related to a special infilling of the Holy Spirit. Believers in whom the Spirit dwells are given a special measure of the Spirit to proclaim the mighty works of God.

The sharing of everything by the first disciples (verses 32 to 37)

Most people are painfully aware of the great gulf which exists between the affluent and the needy in the world today. There is both the disparity between developed countries and underdeveloped countries and between the prosperous and the poor in the developed countries themselves. We are told that some two million Australians live below the poverty line.

What can Christians do when faced with these ugly details? Is it wrong to own two cars and a nice home, have children at private schools when millions go to bed each night hungry and cold? Perhaps Acts 2, verses 44 to 45 and Acts 4, verses 32 to 37, which speak of the sharing of possessions and the generosity of the rich, may help us answer these questions.

In verses 32 to 37 we have an elaboration on what is briefly mentioned in chapter 2. We are told that the first Christians held 'all things in common'. They were united in faith, love and in the sharing of their possessions. As a result, 'there was not a needy person among them' (verse 34). Those who had possessions or lands sold them and gave the proceeds to the apostles for distribution. Joseph, a Levite, a native of Cyprus, who was given the name 'Barnabas' or 'son of encouragement', is singled out as an example. Presumably, he was always encouraging other believers.

What do we learn for today's Christian living from these stories about the wealth sharing of the first Christians? Some have suggested that Luke is advocating a kind of Christian communism — the common ownership of all possessions within the Christian family. But as Luke does not mention this matter again and the common ownership of possessions is not advocated elsewhere in the New Testament, this can hardly be the case. It would seem rather that Luke is simply recounting what he had heard took place amongst the earliest Christians to illustrate the transforming power of the Holy Spirit.

From these two accounts of the sharing of possessions, we learn that this is what happens when the Holy Spirit awakens social consciousness and changes people's attitudes to the things they possess:

* *First*, Christians develop an active sense of responsibility for each other. They put into practice Jesus' command to 'love one another as I have loved you' (John 15, verse 12).
* *Second*, Christians have a real desire to share from their abundance with those in need. The Bible does not ask Christians to give away everything or commend poverty. There are, however, many warnings about self-indulgence at the expense of those in need and about how riches can blind our eyes and dull our consciences.[2]

* *Third*, Christians are to give willingly, sacrificially and gladly. We must note that the sharing of possessions and wealth by these early Christians was completely voluntary. It was spontaneous. There is no law for Christians on how much we should give or, for that matter, on how much we should keep to spend on ourselves. Each one of us has to struggle with this matter before God.

Discussion questions

Talking it through

1 What changes had taken place in Peter and John since the days when they were with Jesus? What had caused these changes?

2 Explain what 'boldness' means in each of the following situations:
   (a) a soldier attacking an enemy in battle
   (b) a student being cheeky to a teacher
   (c) a staff member flirting with someone of the opposite sex.

How would you describe Peter and John's 'boldness'?

3 If prayer is 'God and supplicants aiming for the same goal', how can verses 23 to 31 be seen as true prayer?

4 How is the sharing pattern of behaviour in verses 32 to 37 linked with the words and actions of the earlier part of the chapter?

Widening our horizons

1 Whom or what do you see as the source of evil in the following situations:
  (a) a husband's physical cruelty towards his wife
  (b) epilepsy and fits
  (c) expressions of anger when a person's position of dominance is threatened?
  Does it really matter who/what is responsible?

2 Look at the lives of these influential Christians down the ages. Does it tell us anything important about the types of people God chooses for his work?
  (a) Francis of Assisi
  (b) Mother Theresa of Calcutta
  (c) John Newton, slave trader and preacher

3 Do you see the following as inappropriate or incompatible behaviour for Christians in the light of the grinding poverty of the world:
  (a) having children at expensive schools
  (b) owning two cars

(c) going on an overseas trip?

Justify your position with more than reasons of social status, personal convenience or individual choice (I am/I need/I want this!).

4 What merit has each of the following from a Christian viewpoint:
(a) having a common purse for a Christian community
(b) making a vow of poverty in a monastic order
(c) making ethical investments
(d) being a member of a 'faith mission'?

5
Threats from without and within

ACTS CHAPTER 5

PERSECUTION IS ONE MEANS the devil uses to undermine the gospel. In Acts 3 and 4 and in the second half of Acts 5 we read of the opposition he stirred up against the leaders of the early Christians in Jerusalem.

In the first part of Acts 5 we read of another kind of attack. In this incident, the devil tries to thwart the advance of the gospel by leading members of the church into sin. He raises up people who profess, but do not practise; who want the praise of others more than the praise of God.

Such problems within the church are not unknown — famous TV evangelists who fall into sin, the ordained minister who is unfaithful to his wife, the church treasurer who absconds with the funds, the organist who molests a choir boy, the leading Christian layman who is dishonest in business or public office.

How is it, we ask, that people can so defame the name of Christ? Are they hypocrites who have never really believed in Christ, or are they Christians who have fallen and fallen badly? And when such things happen, how should the church as an institution respond? Are these people to be repudiated and excluded from the life of the church, or should they, on repentance, be accepted back? And what of those who hold high office? Should an ordained minister be given a second chance?

The answer to such questions is by no means straightforward. Each particular case needs to be considered on its own merits. In the past, it seems the church has often been too harsh and allowed for no mercy, whereas in the present, the policy seems to be almost too lenient, as if public sins do not really matter too much. Acts 5, verses 1 to 11 raises an example of public sin in the church. Although this story is about specific people and a particular sin and therefore cannot teach a universal rule, it does demonstrate how seriously God takes public sin in the church.

Three scenes give content to this chapter. The first story is about the judgment of Ananias and Sapphira. This completes the account of the sharing of possessions begun in chapter 4. Barnabas is cited as a good example; Ananias and Sapphira as a bad example. Then follows a brief Lucan summary in verses 12 to 16 describing the continuing growth and activities of the Christian community. The final scene in verses 17 to 42 recounts the arrest of the apostles, their trial and eventual release.

The danger of lying to God
(verses 1 to 11)

The contrast with what Luke has just recounted in Acts 4, verses 32 to 37 is noted by the opening 'But' found in most translations in verse 1. Ananias and Sapphira were of a very different calibre to Barnabas. They sold a piece of land, kept some of the proceeds, and then claimed they had surrendered all. Their sin was not in keeping a proportion, but in *lying* about the money. This lie Peter takes as a lie to the Holy Spirit (verse 3) and to God (verse 4). Peter understands that this sin was evoked by the devil leading Ananias astray.

Peter does not call down judgment on Ananias, but the shock of the revelation of his sin by Peter is so great that Ananias falls down dead. Perhaps he had a stroke or a heart attack. The immediate causes may have been natural ones, but the ultimate cause was, of course, God. Ananias experienced the immediate judgment of God on his sins. No wonder, Luke says, 'great fear came upon all who heard it' (verse 5).

About three hours later, Sapphira arrives, not knowing what has happened. She, too, lies about the sale. Peter confronts her with her sin and tells her of her husband's death. On hearing this, Sapphira also drops down dead.

This story, so very difficult for the modern mind to comprehend, teaches two important lessons. One is that the Christian community is never perfect. Even in these early heady days, immediately after Pentecost, members of the church failed and failed badly. The second is that God takes deliberate sin very seriously. The writer of the book of Hebrews underlines this point. He constantly warns against deliberately provoking God, for he says, 'It is a fearful thing to fall into the hands of the living God' (Hebrews 10, verse 1).

The motive behind Ananias' and Sapphira's sin should also be noted. They made their public gift because they wanted the praise of others. By pretending to give sacrificially, they sought to be numbered with such people as Barnabas and gain personal prestige within the church. As John Stott says, 'their motive in giving was not to relieve the poor, but to fatten their own ego.'[1]

The continuing growth of the Christian community (verses 12 to 16)

In this brief Lucan summary, the ability of the apostles to heal in the name of the Lord and the continuing growth of the number of believers is mentioned. 'The rest' (verse 13) refers to unbelievers. In the light of the power evident amongst the Christians, their opponents kept away.

The second arrest, trial and release of the apostles (verses 17 to 32)

The reaction of the Jewish leaders to all this activity is strikingly similar to what Luke recounts in Acts 4. The same pattern emerges. The apostles preach, heal and large numbers respond. Then the Jewish authorities intervene.

In the first arrest, only Peter and John were imprisoned, but this time it is all the apostles (verse 18). What is more, on this occasion an angel miraculously releases the apostles and sends them back to the temple to continue their preaching (verses 19 and 20). Not surprisingly, the Jewish rulers are amazed to hear that the prisoners have escaped and are once more preaching. They thus send for them to be brought before the Sanhedrin.

The Jewish rulers remind the apostles of their former directions to desist from preaching, but Peter and the others respond, 'We must obey God rather than any human authority' (verse 29). They simply cannot obey such a command no matter who gives it. This confrontation allows the apostles once more to tell the Jewish rulers that they were in error in crucifying Jesus and that he has now been exalted and offers repentance and the forgiveness of sins (verses 30 to 32).

This speech enrages the Jewish rulers and some of them want the apostles killed (verse 33). Gamaliel, a great Pharisaic teacher of the Law, however, privately counsels otherwise. He notes that other mass movements such as the ones led by Theudas and Judas quickly collapsed (verses 36 and 37) as they were not of God. He adds that if this movement is of human origin it will also fail, but if of God, no opposition will destroy it (verses 38 and 39).

What is more, if it is of God, to oppose it would be to oppose God. The decision is made therefore to flog the apostles, to forbid them to speak in the name of Jesus and then to let them go (verse 40). The apostles leave rejoicing and take up their preaching again.

These stories of persecution remind us that opposition to the preaching of the gospel seldom succeeds. History shows us that time and time again, God turns opposition and persecution into a powerful instrument to awaken the church and give new impetus to the mission. These early Christians faced impossible odds, but Christ's presence was so *real* that they felt *compelled* to speak and preach of Jesus, their resurrected and ascended Lord.

Closed and open churches

The story of Ananias and Sapphira and that of other Christians who have committed public sins, raises the question of church discipline. Should Christians try to ensure that only genuine believers who are without moral fault be allowed as church members, or should the doors of the church (metaphorically speaking) be kept wide open?

In the early church, high standards were maintained. Jesus said an unrepentant sinner should be excluded from the church (Matthew 18, verse 17) and Paul taught something similar (1 Corinthians 5, verses 1 to 7), but with the passing of time a more lax approach developed. As the church grew in numbers, it was impossible to know what everyone was doing and, when strict rules were enforced, some other sins, equally serious, were ignored.

In today's world, the mainline churches have basically abdicated responsibility in this area. What they could do is by no means clear. As Christians tend to come and go as they please if one congregation or denomination sets rules or singles out someone, anyone affected can simply leave and expect to be welcomed somewhere else. This is said not to commend or criticise this fact, but only to highlight the reality.

There are, however, churches even today which maintain a very strong discipline. I am friendly with someone who was excommunicated from a closed Brethren chapel because he disobeyed a church law that forbade university attendance. He is now married and has children, but his parents who still belong to the church are not allowed to speak to him, his wife or their grandchildren. This is surely a case of misguided discipline.

The Roman Catholic Church practises discipline on a selective basis. Those who remarry without the church's permission, 'pro-choice' activists — such as

Catholics for Abortion — and priests who leave the church and marry are the ones usually singled out. What we might call public sins — such as that of Ananias and Sapphira — seem to gain no official reaction.

We see from all this that no easy answer is possible, but if the church is too lax it can undermine all that it stands for. The story of Ananias and Sapphira does not offer a solution, but it does remind us that public sins in the life of the church are a great offence to God. We should never forget this.

Discussion questions

Talking it through

1 What or who brought about Ananias and Sapphira's death?

2 What does the Ananias and Sapphira story reveal about God's attitude to sin? Why do you suppose such an attitude was taken here and not in other similar cases? Do worse things happen today?

3 Is there a connection between the growth of the church in verses 12 to 16 and the Ananias and Sapphira story?

4 Should the church be confined to the morally pure?

Widening our horizons

1 Is it right to shrug our shoulders and say certain sins inevitably have certain outcomes in such cases as Ananias and Sapphira? What is your attitude to the following:
(a) the sudden death of a person consumed by ambition who dies from stress
(b) the distress of workaholic parents whose children have become drug-dependent
(c) the death from cancer of a treasurer two years after being sacked for embezzling church funds?
What role should compassion play?

2 Do you have a problem with any of the following? What is your position or point of view?
(a) 'Expensive research into curing AIDS should be abandoned because it is God's judgment on behaviour that's made them HIV-positive.'
(b) 'Social welfare assistance should be terminated for the unemployed — their problems are God's judgment on their laziness.'

(c) 'TV evangelists who morally fail deserve what is coming to them — God judges hypocrites.'

3 Do you see Peter's response (verse 29) to the Jewish rulers' instruction that they shouldn't preach as an overreaction? Do a little historical research and comment on similar statements by:
(a) Polycarp
(b) Martin Luther
(c) the sixteenth century Anabaptists
(d) Archbishop Oscar Romero.
Is there any other way out in such situations?

4 You are on a church committee recommending forms of church discipline for your church. Some of the problems you are faced with are:
(a) the open practice of adultery by a couple in the congregation
(b) apparently irreconcilable differences between two members of the congregation
(c) a member who is a local alderman and is reported to favour his own business interests in council.
What course of action do you recommend in each case?

6
Leadership in the new community

ACTS CHAPTER 6

THIS CHAPTER BEGINS a new section of the book. The first five chapters have described how the Christian community in Jerusalem began and expanded under the leadership of the twelve apostles despite persecution from the Jewish leaders. In chapters 6 to 9, Luke tells how other Christian leaders arose and the mission moved beyond the confines of Jerusalem.

In this extended section we read of the appointment of the seven (verses 1 to 6); the rise of Stephen to prominence (verses 8 to 15); the martyrdom of Stephen (chapter 7); the ministry of Philip (chapter 8, verses 1 to 40) and of the conversion of Paul (chapter 9, verses 1 to 31).

How church leaders first emerged
(verses 1 to 7)

Each one of the present-day denominations has a special title for its ministers — pastor, priest, rector, preacher — and it is often suggested that the way 'our church' organises itself is the biblical pattern. But what we find when we read the New Testament historically (rather than dogmatically) is that patterns of congregational leadership slowly developed and took various forms from place to place.[1]

In Acts 6, verses 1 to 6 we catch a glimpse of one of the very earliest steps made to organise the church's leadership. I use the word 'glimpse' deliberately, for Luke gives this story to introduce Stephen, not to explain how church leadership developed.

It would appear that in the early days, the twelve apostles gave leadership to the Jewish Christian community in Jerusalem, mainly on the basis of their privileged status as the chosen and personally taught disciples of Jesus, although their main function was to bear witness to the life, teaching, death and resurrection of Jesus. In the small house churches into which the ever-growing number of disciples in Jerusalem were divided, other leaders emerged. Probably the owner of the homes in which the Christians met usually gave the lead, although widespread interaction and sharing seems to have been the norm at first (see 1 Corinthians 14, verse 26).

As the leadership of the whole Christian community does not seem to have been understood as the continuing responsibility of the twelve, Luke suggests that others took over this work. Although Luke in verses 1 to 6 makes the seven responsible solely for the care of the food distribution to the Hellenist widows, he may be implying that in fact they were appointed as the communal leaders of the Hellenist Christians.

Later, Luke has just one group of elders — older Christians — as the communal leaders of all the Christians in Jerusalem. This governing body, eventually under the chairmanship of James — Jesus' brother but not one of the twelve — seems to have replaced both the twelve and the seven.[2] If this is so, it suggests that as time passed the divisions were overcome.

The term 'Hellenist', in this context, means a Greek-speaking Jew. The term 'Hebrew' means a Hebrew or Aramaic-speaking Jew. The language difference, as is often the case, caused division in the Christian community. The Hellenist Christians thought their widows were being neglected in the daily distribution of food, supervised by the Hebrew-speaking apostles. Widows in such a male-dominated age were amongst the most needy, for without a man there was no means of support. The early Christians apparently made sure no Christian widow was in need (see Acts 4, verse 34).

In the face of this dissension, the apostles call the whole community together and suggest a solution.

They declare, 'It is not right that we should neglect the word of God to wait on tables' (verse 2). Distributing food is the specific problem, but the general superintendence of the community is the real issue. The community accepts this principle. To do the work, they suggest, 'seven men of good standing, full of the Spirit and of wisdom' (verse 3) should be appointed.

The use of the term 'full' in relation to Spirit and wisdom is important to note. In neither case is the word used in an absolute sense. There was to be evidence of the Holy Spirit at work and spiritual wisdom. These were needed in full measure, but growth was still possible.

Seven men were chosen, all of them Hellenists. From then on, the material care of the Hellenist widows, and possibly the general oversight of the Hellenist Christians, was their responsibility.

These seven are not called 'deacons'. This is important to note because church tradition often refers to the seven as the first deacons. The verb 'to serve' or 'to minister' — in Greek, a form of the noun transliterated into English as 'deacon' — is used both of the work of the apostles who give themselves to preaching and prayer *and* of the work of the seven. In other words, both preaching and administration/caring are here seen as Christian service or ministry.

The seven take up their work after the whole church has prayed for them, laying their hands upon them (verse 6). This was a solemn act of public commissioning of those selected by the community to hold office.

Following the resolution of this problem, Luke in a little summary comment (verse 7) tells of the continuing growth in the number of disciples. Amongst the converts, he notes, there were many Jewish priests. On becoming Christians they lost their special status as priests, for in the new community every believer had free access to God and the whole body of believers was seen as a priestly community.[3]

What we see in this story is a very early division in ministry: some are to concentrate on the ministry of the word, others on the ministry of practical service. In 1 Peter 4, verses 10 and 11 we see exactly this same division. What follows in Acts shows, however, that to concentrate on one of these ministries did not exclude a person from the other ministry.

The qualities of Stephen, a church leader (verses 8 to 15)

Now that Luke has told how Stephen came to prominence, he introduces him more fully before giving an account of his actions which led to his martyrdom. Here Stephen is shown to be far more than one of a group who simply distributes food to the widows. He is described, like the apostles, as a man 'full of grace and power [who] did great wonders and signs among the people'.[4] So powerful was his ministry that, like the apostles, he soon was opposed.

The opposition is said to have come from some who belonged to the synagogue of the Freedmen and the Cyrenians, the Alexandrians, and those from Cilicia and Asia. Some scholars think Luke refers to five different synagogues (one for each group), while others such as F.F. Bruce think only two synagogues are implied, that of 'the Freedmen', Jewish men who had once been slaves, and that of the group of nationals listed.

The number does not matter, but what this verse discloses is important. In Jerusalem, there were many synagogues — the Rabbinic writings say over 400 in number. These were gatherings of like-minded Jews, consisting of at least ten men, who in most cases met in homes like the early Christians did. In other words, in meeting in homes in small groups, the early Christians followed Jewish practice.

In Luke's account of Stephen's speech, recorded in Acts 7, Stephen makes a stinging attack on the Jews. As a Hellenistic Jew converted to Christianity, Stephen may well have represented a more radical response to the Law and Jewish traditions than that espoused by the earliest Jewish Christians.

In the light of this possibility, we should note the charge made against him: 'We have heard him speak blasphemous words against Moses and God' (Acts 6, verses 11, 13 and 14).

The force of the Jewish Law for Christians was a

matter of dispute and contention among the first believers.[5] Some Jewish Christians wanted the Law's demands enforced as necessary for salvation, but in the end it was agreed that, while Jewish Christians could and perhaps should keep the Law, salvation was entirely by grace. Jew and Gentile were saved solely on the basis of what Christ had done on the cross which was received by faith. No amount of law-keeping or good works could earn salvation.[6]

The early house churches

In the first century and well into the second century, the main meeting place for Christians was usually a larger-than-average home. It was, in fact, not until the fourth century that special Christian buildings became common. The homes used were invariably provided by a person of some social standing and substance who was a firm believer himself as were all of his household. Into this extended family which included not only grown-up children but also servants and often slaves, other Christians were added.

Comments about Christians meeting in homes are quite common in Acts[7] as they are in Paul's writings.

Usually the host of these home churches would have been a man, but the number of women 'heads of homes' who host churches is quite significant.[8]

It would seem that at first these house church hosts, who would have given some general oversight when the Christians gathered together, had no special title,[9] but with the passing of time they came to be called *episkopos* —which can be translated as 'overseer', 'superintendent' or 'bishop'. Those who helped them in generally serving the church were called *diakonoi*, which can be translated 'minister', 'servant' or 'deacon' (see Philippians 1, verse 1 and 1 Timothy 3, verses 1 to 12 — the only two places in the New Testament where the titles are mentioned together).

The house church setting for early Christian worship determined, to some extent, the character of community life. A house setting is a far more intimate context than a large, specially built building. Sharing together, informality and responsive and interactive leadership all would have been encouraged. In these gatherings, a meal was usually eaten together and, as part of this, a cup and bread were set aside for celebration of holy communion (or 'holy fellowship' — the terms mean the same) which later was called 'a thanksgiving' (*Eucharist*).[10]

In recent years, thousands of Christians have tried to regain this quality of communal life by joining a home church or home fellowship, usually while still affiliated to a large congregation which meets on Sundays. When this is the pattern, the two different kinds of Christian gatherings complement each other.

Discussion questions

Talking it through

1 Why did the pattern of leadership change from time to time in the early church? How flexible was it?

2 Why did Jewish priests lose their special status when they became Christians?

3 What is 'grace' (a dictionary definition would be fine)? How does it differ from the Jewish law?

4 What aspects of Christian teaching about relationships were particularly well-catered-for in the house church setting of the first century? How can this quality of mutual caring and support be maintained today?

Widening our horizons

1 What kind of leaders should we expect for the followers of a teacher who washed his disciples' feet? In what areas of corporate life are the following most appropriate/not appropriate:
(a) decision-making by the bishop, priest or minister
(b) decision-making by the ruling elders
(c) decision-making by the total church membership?

Are there ever occasions when people ought to do something just because the leader says so?

2 Church growth experts often draw on a business or corporate model for life in the Christian community. How useful are the following models of leadership:
(a) a company managing director
(b) a business consultant
(c) a parent
(d) a sporting coach
(e) an encounter group facilitator?

3 In what ways do each of the following patterns of congregational gathering fit in with twentieth century life:
  (a) the Christian Life Centre and such large-scale churches
  (b) the traditional parish church
  (c) the informal house church?

4 What makes for community? How do you think a mature Christian community should cope with each of the following:
  (a) a family suddenly deserted by the breadwinner
  (b) an old person with Alzheimer's disease
  (c) a mentally retarded adult?

  Should the local church always be a community in this sense, or is this expecting too much of people who only see each other once or twice a week?

7
A spirited defence of the community's beliefs

ACTS CHAPTER 7

JESUS WAS BORN TO DEVOUT Jewish parents, he was raised in his ancestral faith, he revered the Jewish scriptures, all his disciples were Jews, his earthly ministry was almost entirely directed to Jewish people — yet after his resurrection he sent his followers out to preach the gospel 'to the end of the earth', to the Gentiles (Acts 1, verse 8; see also Matthew 28, verse 19).

Not surprisingly, one of the most difficult questions the early Christians had to work out was the relationship between Judaism and Christianity. Was Christianity a completely new religion, a total break with Judaism? Or was it simply the old religion divided between those who recognised Jesus as the Messiah and those who did not? Or was the relationship even more complex than either of these stark alternatives suggest? The last option seems to be the case.

Luke in writing Acts is struggling with these questions. In his distinctive way he provides both an historical and a theological explanation. As an historian, he tells how in fact the early Christians did break with Judaism as more and more Gentiles came to believe in Christ. As a theologian, he argues that this is what the Old Testament predicted would happen. The inclusion of Gentiles into a restored Israel, ruled by the Messiah and vivified by the Spirit, was God's eternal plan for the redemption of the world. The believing Christian community is a new reality, but its roots lie in Judaism: the Old Testament prepared the way for the New.

Luke's boldest statement of the change initiated by God himself appears in Stephen's speech. Here we are told God is about to pass by stiff-necked Jews and call out a new chosen people made up of Spirit-filled believers in Christ. On first reading, the speech or sermon seems to be a long-winded, wandering recital of parts of the Old Testament which ends in a bitter attack on the Jews. It is the kind of chapter in the Bible we quickly pass over. But a little work and thought soon gives meaning and purpose to this section of Acts.

Stephen points out that God had raised up a

whole series of deliverers for his people Israel and Jesus was the culminating one; that they had disobeyed the Law which had been given to guide them; that they had mistakenly thought the tabernacle — the tent of meeting in the wilderness — and the temple were homes in which God dwelt. Stephen does not actually say, 'and now God has rejected you', but this is *implied*.

The speech comes just before the worldwide mission begins. Stephen's words provided the theology for this mission and the persecution which followed his death provided the impetus for the early church to take it on.

Stephen's review of Israel's history

Stephen's speech picks up four major epochs in Israel's history, dominated by four major characters: Abraham, Joseph, Moses and David. The common theme developed is that in the periods of none of these individuals was God's presence limited to any one place. Stephen's point is that the God of the Bible is constantly doing new things and his people must be attentive to his leading.

❑ *Abraham and the patriarchal age*
 (verses 2 to 8)
Abraham is the first to discover that God calls his people to move out in faith. The Lord appears to Abraham not in Canaan but in Mesopotamia, emphasising that God does not restrict his activities to

the land of the Jews.

❏ Joseph and the sojourn in Egypt
   (verses 9 to 16)

Having mentioned the twelve sons of Isaac (verse 8), Stephen singles out the most important of them in the Old Testament story, Joseph. As with Abraham, Stephen notes that God appeared to Joseph outside of Canaan in Egypt. To underline the point, he repeats the word 'Egypt' six times in seven verses.

Joseph is drawn as the deliverer or saviour of his extended family (verse 14). He provides for them and forgives them despite their former rejection and persecution of him. He thus foreshadows the rejection of Jesus by his brethren and the forgiveness he offers.

❏ Moses and the exodus and wilderness
   wanderings (verses 17 to 44)

This section is the longest in the sermon. Verses 17 to 22 tell of Moses' birth in Egypt and how he became part of the royal household. Verses 23 to 29 show that Stephen divides Moses' life into three forty-year periods. Here we read of his middle years when driven out of Egypt. The point is that although Moses wanted to deliver his people, he was rejected. Verses 30 and 34 point out that after long years in exile, God appears to Moses in a burning bush. He is told to return to Egypt, for through him

God plans to deliver the Jews.

In verses 33 to 43, three main thoughts dominate. The first is the success of Moses in delivering God's people and God's gift of the Law (verses 35 to 38). The second is the failure of the Jews to obey Moses or God's law (verses 39 to 41). The third is that disobedience evokes God's displeasure and rejection (verses 42 to 43).

❑ *David and the temple*
   (verses 44 to 50)
In the wilderness, the tabernacle — a large tent surrounded by a holy area — had served as the central place of worship. When the kingdom was established in Canaan, eventually under David, he wanted to build a permanent holy place. He could not do this, but Solomon his son did.

The temple became so important to the Jews that they thought it guaranteed God's presence and protection. This idea had become an inviolable dogma by the time of Jesus.

Stephen rejects this very thought. He insists that 'the Most High does not dwell in houses made with human hands' (verse 48). He tells the Jews that they are wrong in trying to tie God down, to limit his presence to the land of Israel or to restrict his offer of salvation to the Jews.

❏ Stephen's conclusion
(verses 51 to 53)

Stephen ends his selective resume of Israel's history by criticising his audience for repeating the same sins as their forefathers: 'You stiff-necked people, uncircumcised in heart and ears, you are forever opposing the Holy Spirit' (verse 51). There is no failure to apply the message in this sermon!

❏ The outcome of Stephen's message
(verses 54 to 60)

When they heard these words the Jewish crowd rose up in anger, drove Stephen out of the city and stoned him to death. Stephen himself is described in his moment of destiny as 'full of the Holy Spirit' and we are told he was given a vision of Jesus as the Son of Man standing in heaven ready to welcome him (verse 56). Like his master Jesus, Stephen prays that God will receive his spirit and that he will forgive his executioners (verses 59 and 60). Saul is said to have been present.

Conclusion

If we had been in Jerusalem at that time, we would have said, 'What a tragedy... How could God take such a gifted preacher in the prime of his life?' Yet from our vantage point, we can see that, if Stephen had not spoken out so boldly, the early Christians might not have seen so clearly that Judaism had had its day. The mission to the whole world might not have begun with such vigour and purpose. Saul might not have been challenged to the very core of his being and soon so radically converted.

When caught up in the events of life, it is often hard to see God's hand at work. Stephen's martyrdom was a human tragedy, but in the overall plan of God it played a very significant part. We can see that today. As one of the early Church Fathers, Tertullian, said: 'The blood of the martyrs is the seed of the church.'

Discussion questions

Talking it through

1 In what ways is Christianity Jewish and in what ways is it something new?

2 What is it about God that makes it nonsensical to think of him as confined to one place? Given this, what do you know of the ancient Jews and their environment that explains how they might be tempted to think of God in this way?

3 Why do you think Stephen chose Abraham, Moses, Joseph and David as his key examples? How did they help his case against Israel?

4 Was Stephen's message a success? You might look at Acts 1, verse 8 and Acts 8, verses 1 to 3 in your answer.

Widening our horizons

1 Christianity has changed since the first century. Many of the more obvious Jewish features, for instance, have dropped out. What sort of flexibility is desirable today amongst Christians in each of these areas:
(a) forms of worship
(b) teaching methods
(c) sexual behaviour
(d) doctrinal innovation?

What are some underlying principles we should follow?

2 What is 'anthropomorphism'? How are the following statements anthropomorphic?
(a) 'God is the God of the Jews — others have their own gods!'
(b) 'This is God's house.'
(c) 'God needs lots of helpers.'
(d) 'By reading the Bible and praying every day, we can know how God thinks.'
(e) 'God needs our love.'

3 If Stephen's sermon has power, its power lies in the story. Tell or write a story of your own that would be applicable to any one of these situations:
(a) You are asked to justify honesty in financial transactions.
(b) You are asked to explain your relationship with God.
(c) You are asked to justify the institution of marriage.
Why are stories such powerful vehicles?

4 Mostly we cannot see the good results of calamitous events. But sometimes we can. Do we see any good having come out of each of the following horrific events:
(a) the Holocaust
(b) the persecution of the early church
(c) the resistance of the churches of eastern Europe to Soviet power
(d) the martyrdom of Christians down through the ages
(e) the suffering of the church in lands of oppression today?
Does this justify the suffering?

8
The spreading of the gospel

ACTS CHAPTER 8

EVERY CHRISTIAN WOULD LIKE to have a more personal relationship with Jesus and know more of the power of the Holy Spirit. We are all conscious of our failures to live robust Christian lives: we don't pray as we should, we find witnessing difficult, we often let Christ down by how we behave.

In the history of the Christian church, it has often been suggested that there is available a 'second work of grace' whereby we can move onto a higher level of spirituality and victory. This is called the doctrine of 'the second blessing'.

In this century, it has been popularised by the Pentecostal movement which holds that all Christians need a second experience called 'the baptism of the Holy Spirit' which is evidenced by the ability to speak in tongues. The scriptural support for this second experience is often found in Acts 8, verses 14 to 16. The Samaritans believed and were baptised, but only later was the Holy Spirit given. Is this a paradigm of how God wills to work in every believer's life? We will need to keep this question in mind as we proceed.

Persecution and its consequences
(verses 1 to 3)
Until this juncture, the proclamation of the gospel has been confined to Jerusalem, despite the fact that the risen Lord's final instructions in Acts 1, verse 8 were that the disciples should be witnesses in Jerusalem and in all Judea and Samaria and to the ends of the earth. Compliance with this command only eventuated when a great persecution of the early Christians erupted after Stephen's death. Saul, who is to become Paul the apostle, seems to have led this onslaught (verse 3). This persecution drove out the disciples, except for the apostles, and they began to preach the word in the surrounding regions of Jerusalem.

Philip and the Samaritans
(verses 4 to 24)
One of those driven out who began to witness to Christ is Philip, who earlier had been appointed to care for the Hellenist widows (Acts 6, verses 1 to 6).

Later, he was called 'Philip the evangelist' (Acts 21, verse 8). He went to a city in Samaria and 'preached the word' (Acts 8, verse 4). A multitude believed when they heard Philip and saw the signs he performed (verse 6). Even Simon, a powerful wonderworker (a religious guru who performed miracles), believed and was baptised (verse 13). So far so good, but what follows is quite unexpected.

When the apostles in Jerusalem heard that Samaritans had believed, they sent Peter and John. Why were they sent? Did they have to check on Philip's work? If so, why only in this case? Equally perplexing is the situation described. When the apostles arrived, we are told 'they prayed for them that they might receive the Holy Spirit, because the Holy Spirit had not yet come upon any of them; they had simply been baptised in the name of the Lord Jesus' (Acts 8, verses 14 and 15, NIV). Why was the Holy Spirit not given when they believed and were baptised as we would expect?

When the reception of the Spirit is mentioned elsewhere in Acts, it is associated with initial belief and water baptism.[1] The story of the group in Ephesus (Acts 19, verses 1 to 7) is not an exception. They are disciples of John the Baptist who have never heard of the Holy Spirit. It is when they believe in Christ that they receive the Spirit. Paul in his own writings is quite emphatic. He says that you cannot claim to be a Christian unless you have received the Holy Spirit (Romans 8, verse 9).

Several solutions to this problem have been given. One is that the Samaritans and Simon were not really converted. Peter and John's visit marked the point when they really believed and thus received the Spirit. Simon's blasphemous suggestion that he be given power to dispense the Spirit is cited as evidence (Acts 8, verses 18 to 23). We are told this shows that at least Simon was not really converted. But Luke does speak of the Samaritans and Simon as believing and being baptised (verses 13 and 14) and he implies that Simon repented when denounced by Peter for his presumption (verse 24). No, this solution is not the answer.

A second suggestion, favoured by many Pentecostals and charismatics, is that here we have evidence for a two-stage conversion process. First, the Samaritans believed and were baptised in water and then later they were baptised in the Holy Spirit. However, this solution also has problems.

There is no mention here of the term 'the baptism of the Holy Spirit', nor of tongue-speaking — of which Pentecostals make so much. Furthermore, we must ask, if it was Luke's intent to teach that *everyone* should have a second experience called the baptism of the Holy Spirit, why does he not give other examples like that at Samaria? Elsewhere, as we have noted, believing, water baptism and the reception of the Holy Spirit seem to be simultaneous.

The best solution is simply to see this as a very unusual event. In God's sovereign purposes, he withheld the giving of the Spirit when the first non-Jews believed until two of the apostles were present. Perhaps this was so that none could deny the reality of what had happened. Luke, in fact, underlines that this delay in giving the Spirit was quite exceptional. In a somewhat surprised tone, he says the Samaritans 'had *only* been baptised in the name of the Lord Jesus' (verse 16). What Luke would have expected was belief in Jesus, water baptism and the reception of the Spirit (sometimes called 'Spirit baptism') basically at the same time.

We conclude then that, while there may be many people today in the churches who know little or nothing of the Holy Spirit, either because they have not been converted or because they have not really acknowledged the Lordship of Christ over their lives, this passage does not teach that *everyone* needs to receive the Holy Spirit in power some time after conversion. People often have wonderful experiences of the Spirit subsequent to becoming a Christian, but this does not set a pattern for others. God deals individually with each one of us.

The normal Christian experience is to believe in Jesus, receive the Holy Spirit and steadily develop a relationship with God. If we have a big leap forward in our awareness of the Spirit somewhere along the journey, it simply means that earlier our spiritual life was stunted. We thank God for his goodness in giving us a spurt along, but we don't make our experience the norm for everyone else.

Philip and the Ethiopian eunuch
(verses 25 to 40)

The very vivid story of Philip's later ministry with the Ethiopian eunuch illustrates the point we have just made. The Ethiopian believed and was baptised. The coming of the Spirit is presupposed, not mentioned, as is the case in many other conversion stories in Acts. There is no suggestion that the Ethiopian needed to receive something extra later.

After his ministry in Samaria, north of Jerusalem, Philip moved south and met up with this Ethiopian travelling on the Gaza road. The man was a high official of the Queen of Ethiopia. Like many court officials of that age, he was a eunuch, someone who according to Jewish law was excluded from the inner courts of the temple (see Deuteronomy 23, verse 1). Nevertheless he wanted to worship the one true God (Acts 8, verse 27).

In Jerusalem he must have obtained a copy of the scroll of Isaiah, for this is what he was reading in his chariot (verse 28). Philip joined him and asked whether he could understand what he was reading and the Ethiopian said, 'No'. The passage quoted (verses 32 and 33) is from the great Servant Song of Isaiah 53 which speaks of Jesus as the suffering servant who gives his life as a ransom for many. When the Ethiopian asked of whom the prophet spoke, Philip beginning with this scripture 'proclaimed to him the good news of Jesus' (verse 35). The great man believed the gospel and asked to be baptised then and there. Philip obliged.

The comment about the Holy Spirit 'snatching' Philip away afterwards (verse 39) is unusual. Whether Luke is suggesting he miraculously and suddenly disappeared or is simply using colourful language for Philip's departure is hard to tell.

Perhaps one thought we could keep in mind is that often we need help, like the Ethiopian, to understand the scriptures. Everyone can read a modern translation and learn about Christ, but there are hard parts, for example many of the Old Testament prophecies, where the help of a well-informed person or a good commentary is needed.

Discussion questions

Talking it through

1 Does God seem to follow certain set steps or procedures when people are converted? What does this tell us about people and how they come to God?

2 Which of the three approaches to the conversion of the Samaritans (pages 112 to 113) do you support? Why? If you disagree with all three, what is your alternative?

3 Using Isaiah 53 as a basis, what do you think Philip said about Jesus (verse 35)?

4 What evidence is there here that the Holy Spirit is the main character in this chapter? Do you think this reading is right?

Widening our horizons

1 Important lessons hang upon the story of the Samaritans' conversion. Look at the following aspects of your own life-story and say what 'life rules' can be drawn for these stories:
   (a) the most life-changing experience you have known
   (b) your first meeting with the most important person in your life
   (c) the most devastating experience in your life.

   Is there a danger in basing too much on one experience or single episode in your life?

2 'May your money perish with you, because you thought you could buy the gift of God with money!' (verse 20, NIV). Why do money and ministry often not mix? What goes wrong?

   What are some good principles for keeping our Christian leadership accountable on how they use money for God's work?

3 Trying to offer explanations for events that obviously involve God are always difficult. How would you explain that these are two sides of the same coin:
(a) I choose to follow God; I am chosen by God to follow him.
(b) I believe in Jesus and have been baptised in/with water, but I am also 'baptised by the Holy Spirit'.
(c) Evil and suffering exist in God's world, but a good God is in control of everything?

4 Philip and the Ethiopian official saw the Old Testament (Isaiah 53) as authoritative. In what sense is each of the following authoritative for you:
(a) the Bible
(b) your parents' instructions to you as a child
(c) the law of the land
(d) the words of someone you respect?

How can the appeal to authority be used positively? When is it unhelpful to do so — even destructive?

9
A dramatic entry into the faith

ACTS CHAPTER 9

JOHN HAD GROWN UP IN THE CHURCH — his parents active church members, Sunday school, youth fellowship: there was no time in his life when he could say that he didn't believe and trust in Jesus. When he went to university, he joined a Christian group where people insisted that everyone needed to be 'born again', that everyone needed a 'Damascus Road experience'. He felt confused and wondered whether he really was a Christian.

As we come to study Acts 9, one question before us should be: Does Luke intend us to regard Saul/Paul's conversion as a paradigm for all Christians, or as a unique event? The story is so important for Luke that he recounts it three times, the two other accounts being found in Acts 22, verses 3 to 16, and Acts 26, verses 4 to 18.

One special feature about this story is that it tells not only of Paul's conversion, but also of his commissioning by God to be the missionary *par excellence* to the Gentiles. He is called and commissioned like one of the Old Testament prophets. Paul himself in his own epistles emphasises the commissioning side of his encounter with the risen Christ, rather than its conversion aspect. It was at this time, Paul says, that he was called by the will of God to be the apostle to the Gentiles.[1]

Saul's/Paul's conversion story (verses 1 to 30)

The first two verses relate back to chapter 8, verses 1 to 3, where Saul's persecuting activities are first mentioned. Saul's zeal was without bounds. He saw the Christians as a threat to all that was dear to him in Judaism.

The disciples of Christ are here called those who belong to 'the way' (verse 2).[2] Behind the term lies the Jewish idea that God's people are to follow his way or direction. This is 'the way of salvation' (chapter 16, verse 7) or 'the way of the Lord' (chapter 18, verse 25). The Christian's claim was that God's way was now fully revealed in Jesus Christ. To follow God's way was to follow Jesus, 'the way, the truth and the life' (John 14, verse 6).

A dramatic entry into the faith/121

❏ *The encounter between Jesus and Saul/Paul*
  (verses 3 to 9)

The encounter is related from an observer's perspective. The mention of the bright light and the voice from heaven reminds us of Old Testament stories of special acts of revelation.[3] The glorified Christ accuses Saul of persecuting him. The thought is that he who persecutes one of Jesus' disciples is in fact persecuting Jesus himself.[4]

In this encounter Saul was turned around — this is the literal meaning of the term 'conversion'. The risen Christ confronted Saul and Saul fell to his knees. Those with Saul heard the heavenly voice, but did not see the risen Jesus (verse 7). Saul himself was temporarily blinded by the light. Like a little child, he was led into Damascus.

❏ *Saul/Paul in Damascus*
  (verses 10 to 19)

In Damascus the Lord appeared to a hitherto unknown disciple named Ananias and sent him to Saul. Ananias was told, among other things, that Saul 'is my chosen instrument to carry my name before the Gentiles and their kings and before the people of Israel' (verse 15, NIV). God had unique work for this Saul/Paul: his special call and commissioning points to this. Ananias visited the indicated home, found Saul, laid his hands upon him in prayer and Saul believed ('gains his sight'), received the Holy Spirit and was baptised (verses 17 to 18).

Saul's/Paul's welcome into the fellowship of believers at Damascus (verses 20 to 25)

Immediately following these events, the converted and commissioned Saul began to proclaim Jesus as the Son of God. Instead of entering synagogues to drag out the Christians, he entered them to preach Christ. How amazed the Jews must have been (verse 21). Not surprisingly they plotted to kill him (verses 23 to 25).

Saul's/Paul's return to Jerusalem (verses 26 to 31)

When Saul returned to Jerusalem and attempted to join the disciples, they were all afraid of him. At first they probably thought he was conspiring to trap them. It was Barnabas who befriended him and assured the others of the genuineness of Saul's conversion. Again the Jews plotted to kill him (verse 29). This section of the book of Acts is drawn to an end by a summary statement provided by Luke (verse 31).

In answer to the question: Does everyone need to have an experience like Paul?, the answer is, of course, 'No'. We all need to be assured that Jesus Christ is our master and Lord, but to have had a dramatic conversion experience or even to be able to remember the time we first responded to Jesus is not necessary. Some Christians can tell of extraordinary events associated with their conversion, others can tell you the day, and sometimes even the hour, when they first believed, but many simply know that now they believe but can tell you little more. Jesus said everyone must 'be born again' — that is, be given new life by the Holy Spirit (see John 3, verses 3 to 8) — but he did not say that everyone must have a born-again *experience*.

Every true believer in Christ is born again by the Spirit, but only some Christians are suddenly and dramatically converted and can tell of a Paul-like conversion or of the born-again *experience*. I say Paul-like conversion because in this story, Paul is uniquely called to be the apostle to the Gentiles, spoken to directly in quite specific terms by the risen Jesus and blinded for three days by the light of God's presence. There are no exact parallels to these events.

Peter at Lydda and Joppa
(verses 32 to 43)

Following Saul's conversion and commissioning as the missionary *par excellence* to the Gentiles, Luke brings Peter back into the story. Perhaps he wished to remind his readers that it was actually Peter — the missionary *par excellence* to the Jews — who at God's leading began the Gentile mission.

Before Luke tells of Peter's ministry in Caesarea with Cornelius in chapter 10, he places him in two towns just south of Caesarea. At Lydda, he healed a bedridden man (verses 32 to 35) and at Joppa he raised to life a woman who had died (verses 36 to 42).

The news of these miracles led in both instances to many people turning to Christ (verses 35 and 42). In both cases the miracle occurred in response to the command of Peter, who was using not his own authority but Christ's. The very special characters of these two miracles should be noted. They parallel the wonderful miracles of Jesus himself.

An interesting question is: Why was Dorcas brought back to life? No-one expected or asked that she be brought back to life. When James, one of the inner three among the twelve apostles, was killed in Acts 12, verse 2, he was not brought back to life. No final answer can be given.

All that can be said is that a miracle is by definition something exceptional. If every sick person got well when prayer was offered on their behalf, or the believing dead were always revived, we would not think of these events connected with Peter as miracles. It seems that both mighty miracles were performed to elicit faith in this frontier missionary situation. God's 'hands' are not tied, nor his power diminished, but this is not the way he works every day.

Discussion questions

Talking it through

1 Is a Paul-type 'Damascus Road' experience necessary for everyone? Can people encounter Jesus by other less direct or dramatic routes?

2 Is 'people of the way' a good name for Christians? What particular aspect of being a Christian does such a name suggest?

3 Do Peter's miraculous healings indicate that he had the same powers as Jesus? Compare Acts 9, verses 39 to 41 with Mark 5, verses 38 to 43. Did he have some special status, or were his miraculous powers simply due to God working in him? See John 14, verse 12.

4 Is there a single, simple reason for miracles happening? Is a miracle an admission of failure on God's part? Is it evidence that normal cause and effect is not good enough?

Widening our horizons

1 Paul is here commissioned to be a missionary. Is the role of a missionary the same today as it was then? Comment on whether or not these are 'missionaries':
(a) an industrial chaplain
(b) a Christian teacher in a Third World country
(c) a Bible printer
(d) a Christian working in an office
What is your definition of a missionary?

2 How is Paul's experience of being 'turned around' or 'converted' similar to each of the following:
(a) getting to the end of a detective story and some novels (e.g. Jane Austen, Agatha Christie or P.D. James) and realising that your assumptions about people/circumstances were entirely wrong
(b) abseiling (or skydiving, bungee-jumping or water-skiing) for the first time after swearing for years you would never do so
(c) apologising to someone who has been

your enemy for a very long time?

3 What comment would you make about each of these 'conversions'? Are all equally valid?
 (a) 'I cannot remember a time when I didn't trust Jesus.'
 (b) 'I had a number of so-called "conversions". I don't know when I first became a Christian, but I am sure I am one.'
 (c) 'I suppose I'm a Christian. After all, I go to church — that must mean something.'
 (d) 'I can clearly remember a moment when I came to know Jesus and this transformed my life.'

4 Can the following events be classified as 'miracles':
 (a) a person healed after a seemingly impossible operation
 (b) a person artificially rescuscitated after stopping breathing for some time and having 'after death' experiences
 (c) the reconciliation of seemingly implacable enemies
 (d) the bringing back to life of Dorcas? What, then, is a miracle?

10
Launching the Gentile mission

ACTS CHAPTERS 10 AND 11, VERSES 1 TO 18

THE COMMAND OF THE RISEN CHRIST to go out and preach the gospel to the whole world[1] is the charter for the Gentile mission, but Luke's story of just how this big step actually took place reminds us of the momentous nature of this development.

The first Jewish Christians were, in fact, breaking down all the barriers their national religion had created when they included Gentiles in the Christian community. The Jews despised Gentiles, calling them dogs, and considered them destined for eternal damnation. No orthodox Jew would enter the homes of Gentiles, even God-fearers, or invite them into their home — let alone eat with them (see Acts 10, verse 28).

Religion, ignorance and prejudice all combined negatively in the mind of Jews when they thought of Gentiles. Persecution, the miraculous conversion and commissioning of Saul and a vivid vision to Peter were all needed to launch the Gentile mission. God had to drop a cluster bomb!

Peter sent for by Cornelius
(verses 1 to 8)

Caesarea was the seat of the Roman governor of the province of Judea. It was located on the Mediterranean coast about 100 kilometres north-west of Jerusalem. Herod the Great had rebuilt the city and created a large artificial harbour. Most of the occupying Roman army was stationed at Caesarea.

Cornelius was a centurion — he had authority over a hundred men — in that part of the army made up of Italians. He, together with his family, had become interested in Judaism and was regularly praying to the one true God. Luke calls him a 'God-fearer'. This means he remained Gentile according to the Jewish law and had not been circumcised (Acts 11, verse 3). This is why Peter was reluctant, to say the least, to obey God's call to visit him (see chapter 10, verses 28 and 29).

One day at about three o'clock in the afternoon (Acts 10, verse 3), Cornelius had a vision. He saw clearly an angelic visitor and was told to send men to Joppa to bring Simon called Peter who was staying with Simon the tanner.

Peter's visions (verses 9 to 23)

On the next day, Peter was praying on the roof of Simon's house and he, too, had a vision (verse 9 onwards). In it he saw something like a large tablecloth coming down from heaven containing 'all kinds of animals and reptiles and birds of the air' (chapter 10, verse 12), some of which the Law forbade Jews to eat (verse 13). Three times this happened. While Peter was thinking about all this, Cornelius' servants arrived (verse 17 onwards). Peter was told in another vision to go with them (verses 19 and 20).

Peter preaches to Cornelius and his household (verses 24 to 48)

After the initial welcome and explanations (verses 24 to 33), Peter expounded the Christian message. We may call it a sermon, but we need to remember the group was seated in a home and Peter had all his hearers gathered around. Peter began by declaring that at last he recognised 'that God shows no partiality'. The gospel is to be offered to all. All who seek after God and do right will gladly respond to this message (verse 35).

Taken in isolation, verse 35 could mean every religious and good person is acceptable to God, but the whole of this chapter is about a devout and good man, Cornelius, who has *not* been acceptable, needs to hear the gospel, repent and believe, find the forgiveness of sins and receive the Holy Spirit. The verse thus obviously does not teach universal acceptance, but suggests God offers a universal invitation, which is especially of interest to 'religious people'.

In Peter's sermon, a brief summary of Jesus' ministry, death and resurrection is given. The invitation to faith comes last (verse 43).

While Peter was still speaking, the Holy Spirit fell upon all those listening and they began to speak in other tongues (verse 46). This was audible evidence that the Spirit had come upon the Gentiles. Proof was needed so that none could deny that Gentiles had been accepted by God and incorporated into the Christian community. With this evidence at hand, Peter felt compelled to baptise these new Spirit-filled believers.

The apostles' investigation (chapter 11, verses 1 to 18)

Before Peter could get back to Jerusalem, the news of the baptism of a whole group of Gentiles had been passed on to the other apostles (chapter 11, verse 1). The 'circumcision party', we are told, were very critical of Peter. These were Christians who taught that, to be a Christian, one had to become a Jew first of all and accept circumcision. They had not yet fully understood the radical breach that had been made with historic Israel through the death and resurrection of Jesus.

In Acts 15, verse 1, some of these mistaken Christians came to Antioch and caused a division by teaching that Christ *and* law-keeping were necessary for someone to be acceptable to God. The apostles then called a conference and settled the issue. The conclusion was that the 'yoke of the law' should not be laid upon the neck of believers. For Peter said, 'We shall be saved through the grace of the Lord Jesus as [the Gentiles] will' (Acts 15, verses 10 to 11).

At this first meeting to discuss this issue, recounted in chapter 11, Peter went over what had happened, telling those assembled about the vision and the visit to Cornelius' house. He concluded that it was only when the Spirit came upon Cornelius and his household that he knew God had accepted Gentiles who believed in Jesus Christ.

The importance of these events to us

Reading this story is interesting as a piece of history, but what it says to Christians today is by no means self-evident. We do not question the inclusion of Gentiles into the Christian community, nor ask if the Old Testament law should be kept. These issues have been settled. There are nevertheless important lessons to be learnt from this chapter.

One of these is that the gift of the Holy Spirit is the essence of being a Christian. When Peter saw that these people had been filled with the Spirit, he knew without doubt that God had accepted them. This gift of the Spirit — which in this context Luke calls, amongst other things, 'the baptism of the Spirit' (chapter 11, verse 17) — was the sign that they had believed. It came right at the beginning of their Christian life, even before they received water baptism. This is a very awkward fact for those who insist that the baptism of the Spirit comes some time after conversion and is only known by some Christians.

Another practical point of application to be learned from this passage is that God does not discriminate against any race. The gospel is a universal offer to all people. John Stott believes the passage speaks against discrimination of all kinds in the church and in society. He says: 'The ugly sin of discrimination has kept reappearing in the church; in the form of racism (colour prejudice), nationalism ("my country right or wrong") and sexism (discriminating against women).' He adds that these sins in the church are 'both an obscenity (because offensive to human dignity) and blasphemy (because offensive to God who accepts without discrimination all who repent and believe)'.[2]

Speaking in tongues

Three times in Acts we read of people speaking in tongues.[3] In the first instance, on the day of Pentecost, this tongue-speaking is a proclamation of the mighty works of God in a language not understood by the speaker, but understood by the hearer. It is a miraculous event and one filled with deep symbolism. It represents the bringing together of the races of humankind torn apart by sin; the overcoming of the divisions depicted in the story of the tower of Babel (Genesis 11, verses 1 to 9).

In the other two instances in Acts, so little is said about the tongue-speaking that few conclusions can be drawn. The point of the comment about tongues in both these texts seems to be they were manifested so as to give audible evidence that the Holy Spirit had in fact been given.

Writing to the Corinthian Christians, Paul speaks of a quite different sort of tongue-speaking than seen on the day of Pentecost. It is a congregational ministry in which an interpreter is needed. Paul insists that this ministry is only one of many ministries given to the body of Christ and not every Christian will speak in tongues. When the apostle asks, 'Do all speak in tongues?' (1 Corinthians 12, verse 30), the Greek construction used demands the answer, 'No'. Paul's major theses in 1 Corinthians 12 to 14 is, first, that Christians have differing gifts or ministries, and second, gifts or ministries which speak directly to the mind such as prophecy are more important than gifts which do not address the mind directly such as tongues (1 Corinthians 14, verses 1 to 3, 18 and 19).

In modern-day Pentecostal churches, much is made of tongue-speaking. It is usually made the one certain sign of baptism with the Holy Spirit, understood as a post-conversion, special endowment.

The speaking of tongues is, however, also encouraged as a congregational ministry and for private personal devotion.

Many Christians, not necessarily belonging to Pentecostal churches, speak warmly of the rewards of such speaking in tongues and this raises no problems. We can thank God for all blessings which help us communicate with him. There are nevertheless two matters of contention: the suggestion that *all* should speak in tongues, which contradicts Paul, and that speaking in tongues is the one fundamental indicator of Spirit baptism.

Most of the great Christian leaders across the centuries and many today, such as Billy Graham and John Stott, just to mention two men whose ministries have obviously been blessed by God, have not spoken in tongues. Modern-day speaking in tongues is the free expression of language in a rhythmic incoherent pattern which may be edifying and mediate spiritual realities, but a prayerful, Christlike life is a much surer indicator of endowment by the Holy Spirit.

Many Pentecostals claim their tongue-speaking is, in fact, a foreign language spoken miraculously, but in thousands of hours of taped tongue-speaking, no example of foreign languages has appeared. Linguists tell us that modern-day tongue-speaking is the free repetition of sounds known to the speaker, but not showing the characteristics of a proper language. It is a patterned form of speech without any given meaning.

136/Launching the Gentile mission

For some people, it erupts spontaneously, especially when expected, but for others, speaking in tongues is a learnt skill in which one grows in fluency with practice. Some tongue-speakers find it a continuing help; others who have begun give up after a while, finding no joy or meaning in tongue-speaking. The latter is quite a common experience.[4]

Discussion questions

Talking it through

1 What is the real significance of the story of Cornelius (verses 1 to 9)? Is it about:
   (a) the place of visions
   (b) the importance of prayer
   (c) God's reward for good deeds
   (d) the missionary heart of God?

2 Jesus said that he came not to destroy the law, but to fulfil it (Matthew 5, verse 17). How do you reconcile this teaching with Peter's vision of unclean animals which God permits him to eat (verses 9 to 16)?

3 What lesson does Peter indicate he has learnt in verse 35? What apparent eternal truth did he have to modify?

4 What evidence is there in this chapter to indicate that the events being dealt with were of crucial significance to God? Why were they

138/Launching the Gentile mission

so important in this critical stage of the early church's development?

Widening our horizons

1 Why is prejudice so powerful? In your answer, consider the following:
  (a) The fierce loyalty people have for their favourite football team.
  (b) The opposition to the erection of a mosque in a predominantly white Anglo-Saxon community.
  (c) The intense hatred between rival racial and religious groups — for example, the Serbs and Croats in the Balkans.
  What is the main cause of such prejudice: race, culture, economic threat, mistrust, plain dislike?

2 Dreams and visions play an important role in the Bible. Recall some of your own or those of others and show how they connect the spiritual realm with the everyday. What do they show you:
  (a) about yourself
  (b) about God's way of working in you
  (c) about God's way of working in the world?

3 This chapter is about change — in Peter in particular, but also in the apostles. Why should we be constantly open to change? Is this linked to God being all-knowing but not all-knowable? Why is deep-seated hostility that is racially or culturally based so difficult to eradicate?

4 Consider your own reaction to difficult issues in the Bible, such as tongue-speaking. Are Bible passages where there are no clear-cut answers a worry to you? Do you feel the Bible should be more straightforward? How does this affect your understanding of:
(a) the church
(b) the Bible
(c) God himself?

11
Establishing the Gentile church

ACTS CHAPTER 11, VERSES 19 to 30

THE SPREAD OF THE GOSPEL beyond Palestine and Judaism is now taken a step further. Luke has told us of the conversion of the first 'half-Jews', the Samaritans (chapter 8, verses 4 to 24), the first Gentiles (chapter 10, verses 1 to 48) and at this point he recounts the founding of the first Gentile church in a Gentile city, Antioch (chapter 11, verses 19 to 26).

The rest of Acts, beginning at chapter 13, has the mission to the Gentiles as its main theme and the apostle to the Gentiles, Paul, as its main character. In Romans 1, verse 16, Paul says the gospel was first for the Jews and then the Gentiles. Luke describes on an historical plane how this took place.

In this section, the church as a social entity comes into focus. We have here, however, a picture of a church quite unlike anything we may have experienced: no special building, no ordained ministry, no denominational affiliation and no detailed creed as we know it. What we see is the very first step in the process of the church becoming an institution. What can we learn, therefore, from such a passage? It is clear we can't make the earliest churches a blueprint for church life today, for so much has changed, but we can get a vision of what the church can be like when the Spirit is active and evangelism is a priority.

These comments remind us that Jesus did not prescribe how the church which came into being after his death and resurrection should be organised. The twelve apostles were called and commissioned to bear witness to the ministry, death and resurrection of Jesus, but they and the later missionary apostles, when they gathered the earliest believers into communities, allowed them to develop their own patterns of leadership and forms of worship. What we see, therefore, in the New Testament is development as the years pass and variation between different churches.

Only after many centuries do we find Christians gathering together in special buildings and having one man as their pastor or priest. In the earliest churches, a large home was the usual setting, corporate leadership variously named was the norm and extensive participation by all present was expected.[1]

The meaning of the word 'church'

In this chapter, we are talking about 'the church', but probably no word in Christian circles is so loosely used. In everyday speech, the term is used of special buildings for worship, denominations, the ordained ministry ('he is entering the church'), of an amorphous institution ('Why doesn't the church do something'), to name a few.

In the New Testament the word 'church' (*ekklesia* in Greek) is not used in any of the above ways. When used of Christians, it refers either to a local community of Christians or to all believers.

Thus in Acts, Luke speaks of the church in Jerusalem (chapter 8, verse 11 and chapter 11, verse 22), or of the church in Antioch (chapter 13, verse 1; see chapter 11, verse 26). When he must speak of Christian communities in different locations, he uses the plural 'churches' (chapter 15, verse 41 and chapter 16, verse 5). If you gathered regularly with other Christians in a given place, you were a member of that church.

So Luke speaks of Herod laying violent hands on 'some who belonged to the church [of Jerusalem]' (chapter 12, verse 1). Luke makes his favoured collective term for Christians, 'the disciples', a virtual synonymn of his local usage of the word 'church'. Thus he can speak either of 'the church in Jerusalem' or 'the disciples in Jerusalem' (chapter 9, verse 19; see chapter 21, verse 16), of strengthening the disciples (chapter 14, verse 23) or strengthening the church (chapter 15, verse 41).

Luke, however, can also use the word 'church', *ekklesia*, of all Christians — the complete assembly of those who believe in Christ. In Acts 20, verse 28, the elders are told 'to feed the church of the Lord which he obtained with his own blood'. All those who believe in Christ and receive the benefits of his death are 'the church'.[2] Acts 9, verse 31 is difficult to categorise. The word 'church', *ekklesia*, is in the singular in some early manuscripts and in the plural in others. If in the singular, it alludes to various local churches; if in the plural, to church members dispersed throughout the places named.

The church at Antioch (verses 19 to 26)

The opening verse in this section parallels chapter 8, verses 2 and 24. It was the persecution in Jerusalem which drove out the first missionaries in an ever-widening circle. Luke says that at first the disciples preached only to Jews (verse 19), but he adds that some, whom he describes as Hellenists — Jews, like Stephen, who spoke Greek and were often born outside of Palestine — preached also to Greeks after coming to Antioch, and many believed (verses 20 and 21).

Antioch was a cosmopolitan city about 300 miles north of Jerusalem on the Orontes river, not far from the Mediterranean coast. It was a great trading centre, the capital of the Roman province of Asia, the third largest city of the empire. Antioch was famous for its fine buildings, many of which were temples, and its long, paved boulevard, flanked by a double colonnade with trees and fountains and its street lighting. Here the first predominantly Gentile church was founded, Jesus' followers were first called 'Christians' and the first church-commissioned missionaries were sent out (chapter 13, verses 1 to 3).

Barnabas and Saul (verses 22 to 26)
When the church in Jerusalem heard of the new Gentile converts in Antioch, they sent Barnabas, 'the son of encouragement' (see chapter 4, verse 36). William Barclay describes him as 'the man with the biggest heart in the church'. Luke himself says 'he was a good man, full of the Holy Spirit and of faith' (verse 24).

When he came to Antioch, he was thrilled to see how the grace of God had triumphed in these people's lives. He exhorted them to remain faithful and apparently to be active in evangelism, for Luke adds, 'a great many people were brought to the Lord' (verse 24).

The work was too much for Barnabas, so he travelled north to Tarsus and asked Saul to return with him. For a whole year, they worked amongst the new believers, instructing them in the faith (verse 26). Luke points out that it was first in Antioch that Jesus' disciples were called 'Christians'. Unlike the terms 'the disciples' or 'the brethren', which the believers used of themselves, this was a name unbelievers gave them. It means those who belong to, or follow Christ.

Elders and prophets (verses 27 to 30)

Barnabas and Saul built up the young church in Antioch but, after about a year, they left Antioch as missionaries to go elsewhere (see chapter 13, verses 1 to 3). Part of their work of consolidation in Antioch, as elsewhere, was the encouraging of local leadership.

In this section we meet for the first time in Acts two early kinds of Christian officer-bearers — the elder and the prophet. Previous to this, Luke has only spoken of Jewish elders[3] and of Old Testament prophets.[4] That he can come to speak suddenly of Christian elders and prophets without explanation suggests that there were some close parallels.

We know Jewish elders were older, respected, spiritually mature men who gave general oversight to Jewish communities. They were laymen without any special responsibilities or duties in the synagogues or temple. Prophets, on the other hand, were God's mouthpiece. They spoke the word of God as it was given to them. We assume, therefore, that Luke understands that Christian elders were also older, respected, spiritually mature believers who gave general oversight to Christian communities (see Acts 20, verse 28 where Luke says the elders had been given oversight, or made 'guardians' (RSV), of the flock).

In 1 Timothy 4, verse 14 Paul speaks of 'the council of elders'. There were thus obviously a number of elders for each congregation. Who are their counterparts in today's church? Some argue that the ordained minister fills this role, but this cannot be so, for ministers today usually work alone and have different responsibilities. The Uniting Church in Australia seeks mature, spiritually minded lay people as elders who share with the ordained minister in the pastoral oversight of the congregation. Possibly some Anglican parish councils, though not using the terminology, could also be thought of as councils of elders. Many Baptist congregations have appointed lay elders.

We should note that wherever Luke mentions elders, Christian or Jewish, they are a group. Neither Luke nor Paul has individual elders in charge of churches, nor do they speak of them as 'ministers' as we know them. The preachers in Acts are the apostles and the prophets. In Acts 13, verse 1, the terms 'prophet' and 'teacher' are linked together. A prophet could have a direct revelation of a future event as has Agabus in this story (chapter 11, verse 28), but usually they are described as exhorting and building up the church through their preaching (see Acts 15, verse 32 and 1 Corinthians 14, verse 3). We can thus think of the Christian prophets as Spirit-guided teachers.

Agabus is given a special revelation from God about a famine soon to affect the people of the Roman Empire (verse 28). Luke tells us this was during the reign of Claudius who ruled from AD 41 to 54. Josephus records a great famine in Palestine in AD 46. Probably the prophet looked ahead to this. The young church immediately decided to begin collecting to relieve their Jewish brethren. This demonstrated not only their compassion, but also their sense of oneness in Christ.

The wall of partition between Jew and Gentile had been breached. The gift was sent by Barnabas and Saul who delivered it to the elders of the Christian community in Jerusalem, who apparently by this time had taken over the general superintendence of the community from the apostles.

Prophecy

Prophecy is the most mentioned ministry in the New Testament and Paul makes it the most important ministry after that of the apostle.[5] It is, however, a ministry that the mainline churches tend to ignore or domesticate by equating it with ordinary preaching or social comment — which it is not.

The special character of prophecy is that it is a direct word from God given to a person who then shares it with others. It is always dependent on a personal revelation. A person who is given frequent prophecies comes to be known as a prophet. Many prophets, mostly men, but some women, are mentioned in the Old Testament, but only the prophecies of a select number were preserved and became scripture. These canonical prophets are the counterparts of the New Testament apostles. Paul, in fact, is called by God like one of the Old Testament canonical prophets (in Acts 9, verses 1 to 19) and he speaks of himself as a servant of God as they did (Romans 1, verse 1). The word of a canonical prophet or an apostle is authoritative in a unique sense; all other prophetic words which claim to come from God must be tested.

The testing of prophecy is an important issue in both the Old Testament and the New. People can claim to be sharing what God has revealed, but in fact what they say may come from the devil or vain imagining. In the New Testament the personal character of the individual prophesying is one key test (see Matthew 7, verses 15 to 23). This suggests that people of mature and consistent Christian character are more likely to hear God clearly and accurately than immature or inconsistent believers.

The content is another test. No true prophecy can contradict or question what is already revealed in scripture, or suggest any immoral behaviour. Most prophecies, however, are not so easily tested for they tend to be words of 'edification, encouragement and consolation' (1 Corinthians 14, verse 3). They are personal messages for individuals or Christian communities. Such prophetic messages can only be tested intuitively. The question is: Does this prophecy sound like what God would say to me, or does this sound like what God would say to our church? Because prophecy is so hard to test, the institutional church tends to push it to one side.

The sermon falls into the category of teaching and/or exhortation. It is based on what is already revealed in the Bible. Nevertheless, a sermon can have prophetic content. A preacher can be moved by the Spirit to share what God has apparently revealed. This reminds us that there is no prescribed formula for a prophecy. A prophecy does not need to begin, 'Thus says the Lord', or 'Thus says the Spirit'. Biblical prophecies take many forms and some have introductory sentences and others do not.[6]

Discussion questions

Talking it through

1 How would you define the word 'church'? How does this definition affect what you do on Sundays? Do you find a gap between the ideal (as described in your definition) and the reality (as you experience it)?

2 Why did the gospel spread beyond Jerusalem, as Jesus said it would (Acts 1, verse 8)? What does this tell us about the way God works?

3 What do the tasks performed by 'elders', 'prophets' and so on in the early Christian church indicate about what the church was there for?

4 What is the significance of the Gentile church in Asia Minor collecting money for the Jewish church in Jerusalem (verses 29 to 30)? What does it show about their view of 'church'?

Widening our horizons

1 Just as the church of Acts 11 is not a model in every detail for us today, so the church today is not a model in every detail for the church of the future. How do you think the future church is likely to change:
(a) in use of personnel
(b) in forms of worship
(c) in involvement in one another's lives
(d) in church government
(e) in property matters
(f) in diversity of practice?

2 Can a good case be made out for *not* using the word 'church' in many of its modern ways? How can the misuse of this term undermine our understanding of God's relationship with us? What other words could be used for its modern meanings?

3 A five-year-old who had always been in a house church was shown a beautiful stone National Trust church building and told by his father that it was a 'a church'. He could

Establishing the Gentile church/153

not comprehend this at all. 'Where is everyone?' was his response.
(a) What does he know, in the light of Acts 11, and what has he yet to learn?
(b) What is the dilemma for congregations who are guardians of National Trust 'treasures'?

4 This chapter shows us the first steps in the church becoming an 'institution'. What do you understand by this term? What are the advantages and disadvantages of the following becoming 'institutions':
(a) Christian schools
(b) aid organisations (for example, World Vision, Community Aid Abroad)
(c) para-church organisations?
   Can a case be made out for an institution being as 'un-institutional' as possible?

5 Prophecy is 'a direct word from God given to a person who then shares it with others'. What tests should we apply to the ideas of those who claim to bring a prophetic message to us? Are these any different from the tests we apply to anyone's reliability?

12
Growth despite the odds

ACTS CHAPTER 12

AGAIN WE READ OF PERSECUTION OF THE early Christians and of another martyr — James, the brother of John. James and John were amongst the first disciples called by Jesus. They left fishing to follow him (Mark 1, verses 18 to 20). Because they were so close to Jesus, they once mistakenly asked him if they could have the chief seats in the kingdom of God (Mark 10, verses 35 to 45).

This James is to be distinguished from James the half-brother of Jesus, who became the leader of the Jerusalem Christian community after Peter. He is mentioned in Acts 12, verse 17; chapter 15, verse 13; and chapter 21, verse 18 (see also 1 Corinthians 15, verse 17). He is probably the author of the Letter of James.

These stories in Acts about persecution remind us of just how costly it can be to be a disciple of Christ. Today in affluent Western society, we easily forget this, for persecution or suffering for Christ are virtually unknown.

It is, however, not so everywhere in the world. Christians have suffered much in this century and thousands have been martyred. In what was the Soviet Union, in China, parts of Africa and South America and elsewhere, the pressures on Christians have been very great.

I have never forgotten reading the story of John and Betty Stam, missionaries in China, who were beheaded by the Japanese. The martyrdoms of Stephen and James are but the first lives lost for Christ. One strange paradox is that when the cost is great, the Christian church flourishes and when the cost is negligible, the church languishes.

The persecuting king (verses 1 to 5)

In the New Testament, a number of Herods are mentioned. The most famous is Herod the Great, who ruled from 37 to 4 BC. It was he who plotted to kill the baby Jesus (see Matthew 2, verses 1 to 12). He bequeathed his kingdom to three of his sons, two of whom Luke mentions in his Gospel (see Luke 3, verse 1).

'Herod the King' in Acts 12, verse 1, is a grandson

of Herod the Great. The Romans gave him this title, but to the Jews he was known as Herod Agrippa I. It is his son, Herod Agrippa II, who later debated with Paul and was almost persuaded to believe.[1]

All the Herods were oriental despots who held the power of life and death over their subjects. That Herod Agrippa I put James to death is quite consistent with what we know of him, especially from the Jewish historian Josephus. After James had been killed, he arrested Peter, for he saw such an action pleased the Jews. However, as it was the time of the feast of unleavened bread which was associated with the annual passover, no immediate action could be taken. Peter was simply put in prison under guard (verse 5).

The response of the church in Jerusalem was earnest prayer for Peter's release. The Christians would not have forgotten Peter's two previous imprisonments (Acts 4, verse 3 and chapter 5, verse 18), nor how on the second occasion the Lord had opened the prison doors and set Peter and John free (chapter 5, verse 19).

Praying was all that they could do. On one side there was Herod with all the powers of the state at his disposal and, on the other, a little band of Christians on their knees. The state and the church had opposing aspirations and each called on the weapons at their disposal.

The power of prayer (verses 6 to 11)

Luke emphasises the security with which Peter was guarded (verse 6). Humanly speaking, it was impossible for him to escape. In the morning he would suffer the same fate as James.

Nevertheless, Peter was able to sleep. He could completely trust God whatever the outcome. Later he would die a martyr's death as Jesus had predicted (see John 21, verses 18 and 19), but not now. An angel of the Lord appeared, the chains fell off and Peter was instructed to dress. The guards apparently were put into a deep sleep, for they offered no resistance and the prison doors opened miraculously (verses 7 to 11).

So amazing were these events that Peter wondered if he were dreaming (verse 9).

The place of refuge (verses 12 to 17)

Peter made his way to John Mark's mother's home. This was probably one of the many house churches in Jerusalem. The maid who went to the door was so startled to hear Peter's voice that she forgot to open it and instead ran to tell those gathered for prayer (verses 12 to 14). Eventually Peter gained entry and told them of his miraculous release.

He ascribed the work of the angel to the Lord himself (verse 17a). His instruction was to go and tell James, Jesus' brother, who we infer was by now the leader of the Jerusalem Christians, and the other brethren (verse 17b).

The results of these events
(verses 18 to 23)

When Herod Agrippa I found that Peter had escaped, he ordered the guards put to death. He showed no mercy. Luke tells us he then went to Caesarea on the coast which was his official capital.

The following details about Herod seem somewhat of a digression away from Luke's main interest, the progress of the gospel. They illustrate again Luke's concern to relate secular history and redemptive history.[2]

The comment about Herod's quarrel with the cities of Tyre and Sidon is mentioned, it would seem, to explain that it was on the day their leaders came to settle the differences that Herod orchestrated a great civic event which was intended to magnify his own person. When everyone was gathered, Herod appeared in magnificent robes and made an oration. The crowd responded by crying out, 'The voice of a god, and not of a mortal!' (verse 22). Herod had tempted the Lord once too often and he was struck down and soon died.

We might be inclined to see this as a fanciful story if Josephus had not also recorded this same story in very similar terms. The Jewish historian describes Herod's royal robe, mentioned by Luke, as 'a garment woven completely of silver, so that its texture was indeed wondrous'. He adds that when the first sunrays fell on the silver robe, 'its glitter inspired fear and awe' and the people addressed him as 'god'. Josephus adds, 'The king did neither rebuke them, nor reject their impious flattery.' As a result, the two independent historians agree Herod was struck down and died soon after.

Luke says he was 'eaten by worms' (verse 23) and Josephus says 'a severe pain. . . arose in his belly' which became so acute that he died within five days. Dr Rendle Short in his book, *The Bible and Modern Medicine*, seeks to harmonise these details. He suggests that Herod may have died from 'intestinal worms' which form into a ball and can cause an acute bowel obstruction.

A reason for this chapter (verse 24)

Acts 12, at first thought, seems to move away from the main story. Luke has told of the establishment and consolidation of the church in Antioch and he could have gone straight on to tell of how these Christians sent out the first official missionaries into Asia Minor (chapter 13, verses 1 to 3). Some have even suggested Luke would have been better to have left out this chapter. Why then did he include this material?

Was it to tell how Peter had to eventually leave Jerusalem to escape Herod Agrippa and to introduce James the brother of Jesus as the new leader of the Jerusalem community? Perhaps, but it is a lot of writing to make these points.

Or was it to emphasise the triumph of God's will

which could not be hindered either by the death of one apostle or the imprisonment of another? When God's people are faithful and prayerful, the gospel triumphs and the enemies of God are brought to naught. If this is the reason, then it is disclosed in verse 24 where it says, 'But the word of God continued to advance and gain adherents.'

Despite all that Herod could do, God's will continued to prosper. Lives were changed, churches were founded and believers were strengthened.

Discussion questions

Talking it through

1 What evidence is there in Acts 12, verses 1 to 5 and elsewhere in Acts that the early Christians did *not* see persecution as a good thing? Should we ever avoid persecution? When is active opposition to the gospel inevitable and therefore not to be resisted?

2 Assume you are one of those praying for Peter in verses 5 and 12 to 14. Make up a fictional account of what might have been happening to you as you reacted to events surrounding Peter's return. Is there humour, fear, adoration, doubt, affirmation?

3 Why do you think Luke is anxious to provide apparently irrelevant historical material about Herod in verses 18 to 23? What does this tell us about the nature of the Christian faith?

4 Using verse 24 as a guide and any other information in the first twelve chapters of Acts, what do you think is the purpose of the book? Has the Book of Acts any more than historical interest for you?

Widening our horizons

1 'The blood of the martyrs is the seed of the church' (Tertullian, an early Church Father). Why do you think this is the case? Is there anything in the nature of Christianity that makes it likely to thrive under persecution?

2 Some Christians who are dying of cancer or are experiencing some such serious disease claim that suffering is good because God has sent it. What arguments could be used to counter this point of view?

How can people who are suffering be comforted? Has this any bearing on the whole question of persecution?

3 The Christians in chapter 12 were suffering at the hands of an oriental despot. What is the appropriate response today by subjects who live under similar regimes, as many do, where:
(a) their taxes are used to prop up a corrupt, self-entrenching government
(b) they are forbidden to worship because

the state has a conflicting ideology
(c) they are faced with the prospect of hiding victims of a corrupt government and lying about it?

Try and make up a simple statement about the *limits* of a Christian's duty to the state.

4 Does the end ever justify the means? Consider this in the following cases:
(a) Where I actively seek to be persecuted in order to help promote Christianity.
(b) Where I seek to hasten my death in order to be forever with God in heaven
(c) Where I steal in order to help the needy.
(d) Where I engage in civil violence — for example, at a weapons exhibition or military base — in order to promote peace.

Endnotes

Introduction
1. Colossians 4, verse 14; 2 Timothy 4, verse 11; Philemon 24
2. Hendrickson, 1984
3. Acts 8, verse 29; Acts 10, verse 19; Acts 11, verses 2 and 19
4. Acts 6, verse 3; Acts 5, verse 36
5. Acts 2, verse 17; Acts 20, verse 28
6. Acts 2, verse 38
7. This is apparent in such passages as Acts 2, verse 38 (cf. Luke 24, verse 14); Acts 3, verse 19; Acts 5, verse 31
8. Acts 2 to 6. Note Acts 3, verse 26.
9. See Luke 24, verse 47; Acts 1, from verse 4 onwards; Acts 2, verses 16 to 21; Acts 3, verse 24; Acts 10, verse 43
10. Acts 8, verse 14; Acts 9, verses 17 and 18; Acts 10, verses 44 to 48
11. Acts 2, verses 42 to 47; Acts 4, verses 32 to 37; Acts 6, verses 1 to 6; Acts 11, verses 29 and 30
12. Acts 9, verses 2, 13, 14, 21, 32 and 41; Acts 11, verse 26; Acts 4, verse 32
13. Faber and Faber, 1960
14. William Ramsay, *St Paul the Traveller and Roman Citizen*,

Hodder and Stoughton, 1895, p.8

Chapter 1
1. Luke 22, verse 69; Luke 24, verse 26; Acts 2, verses 29 to 36; Romans 8, verse 34; Ephesians 4, verses 8 to 10; 1 Timothy 3, verse 16
2. See Luke 8, verses 1 to 3; Luke 24, verse 10
3. See Luke 5, verse 16; Luke 6, verse 12; Luke 9, verse 18; Luke 11, verse 13; Luke 22, verse 4; Acts 2, verse 46; Acts 4, verse 24
4. Acts 2, verse 22; Acts 3, verse 12; Acts 4, verse 8; Acts 4, verse 20; Acts 5, verse 29; Acts 10, verse 34

Chapter 2
1. Exodus 23, verse 16; Leviticus 23, verses 15 to 21; Deuteronomy 16, verses 9 to 12
2. See 2 Samuel 22, verse 16; Job 37, verse 10; Ezekiel 13, verse 13

Chapter 3
1. See Acts 2, verses 19, 22 and 43; Acts 4, verse 30; Acts 5, verse 12; Acts 6, verse 8; Acts 7, verse 36; Acts 14, verse 3; Acts 15, verse 12
2. See Acts 9, verses 32 to 34 and 36 to 41; Acts 12, verses 6 to 10; Acts 13, verses 9 to 11; Acts 16, verses 16 to 18
3. See Romans 8, verses 17 and 18; 2 Corinthians 1, verses 5 to 7; Philippians 3, verse 10; Colossians 1, verse 24; 1 Peter 4, verse 13

Chapter 4
1. See Exodus 19, verse 18; Isaiah 6, verse 4; Acts 2, verses 1 to 3
2. See Luke 12, verses 13 to 21; Luke 16, verses 19 to 31; Luke 18, verses 18 to 30; James 5, verses 1 to 6

Chapter 5
1. John Stott, *The Message of Acts*, IVP, 1990, p.110

Chapter 6
1. I describe this process and outline the various forms in my book, *Patterns of Ministry Among the First Christians*.
2. See Acts 11, verse 30; Acts 15, verses 4 and 6; Acts 22; Acts 21, verse 17
3. See Hebrews 1, verses 19 to 25; 1 Peter 2, verses 9 and 10; Revelation 1, verse 6
4. Verse 8. See Acts 2, verse 43; and Acts 4, verse 33
5. See Acts 15, verse 1; Galatians 2, verses 1 to 21
6. See Acts 15, verses 7 to 11; Romans 3, verses 21 to 26; Galatians 2, verse 16; Ephesians 2, verses 8 and 9
7. See Acts 2, verse 46; Acts 5, verse 42; Acts 12, verses 12 to 17; Acts 16, verses 15, and 31 to 34; Romans 16, verses 5 and 23; 1 Corinthians 16, verse 19; Colossians 4, verse 5; Philemon 3
8. See Acts 12, verses 12 to 17; Acts 16, verse 15; Colossians 4, verse 5; probably Phoebe, Romans 16, verses 1 and 2; and Chloe, 1 Corinthians 1, verse 11.
9. See 1 Corinthians 16, verses 15 and 16; 1 Thessalonians 5, verses 12 and 13.
10. For more on this, see Robert Banks, *Going to Church in the First Century*.

Chapter 8
1. See Acts 2, verse 38; Acts 10, verse 44; Acts 11, verse 17

Chapter 9
1. See Romans 1, verse 1; 1 Corinthians 1, verse 1; 1 Corinthians 15, verse 8; Galatians 1, verses 12 to 17; Philippians 3, verses 4 to 7
2. See also Acts 19, verses 9 and 23; Acts 22, verse 4; Acts 24, verses 14 and 22.

3. See Exodus 3, verse 2; Exodus 4, verse 5; Matthew 17, verses 2 to 5.
4. See Matthew 10, verse 40; Matthew 18, verse 5; Mark 9, verse 37; Luke 9, verse 48; Luke 10, verse 16; John 13, verse 20.

Chapter 10
1. Matthew 28, verse 19; Luke 24, verse 47; Acts 1, verse 8
2. John Stott, *The Message of Acts*, p.197
3. Acts 2, verses 3, 4 and 11; Acts 10, verse 46; Acts 19, verse 6
4. J. I. Packer, *Keep in Step with the Spirit*, IVP, 1985

Chapter 11
1. For further information on this see my book, *Patterns of Ministry Among the First Christians*
2. See also Matthew 16, verse 18; Ephesians 1, verse 22; Ephesians 3, verse 10
3. Acts 4, verses 5, 8 and 23; Acts 6, verse 12
4. Acts 2, verse 16; Acts 3, verse 18, and 21 to 25; and Acts 7, verse 42
5. See 1 Corinthians 12, verse 28; 1 Corinthians 14, verses 1 to 3, and 39; Ephesians 2, verse 20.
6. For more on prophets and prophesying see my *Patterns of Ministry*, chapter 6 or David Hill, *New Testament Prophecy*, Marshall, Morgan & Scott, 1979.

Chapter 12
1. See Acts 25, verses 13 to 26 and verse 32
2. See, for instance, Luke 2, verses 1 and 2; Luke 3, verses 1 and 2.

Bibliography

Introductions and verse-by-verse commentaries

F.F. Bruce, *The Book of Acts*, Marshall, Morgan and Scott, 1962.
A solid, historically based commentary on Acts in the New London Commentary series.

F.F. Bruce, *The Acts of the Apostles: Greek Text with Introduction*, Eerdmans, 1990.
This is the third edition of Professor Bruce's classic. The introduction gives a superb coverage of historical and theological issues.

I.H. Marshall, *Acts: An Introduction and Commentary*, IVP, 1980.
An excellent introduction and verse-by-verse commentary.

D.J. Williams, *Acts: New International Biblical Commentary*, Hendrickson, 1990.
A very good commentary by an Australian scholar, based on the New International version of the Bible.

Introductions and homiletic commentaries

W. Barclay, *The Acts of the Apostles*, St Andrew's Press, 1955.
Provides a lot of historical background to Acts.

John Hargreave, *A Guide to Acts*, SPCK, 1990.
A well-written running commentary which tries to show how events and stories in Acts speak to Christians today. Discussion questions are provided.

J.R.W. Stott, *The Message of Acts*, IVP, 1990.
A series of masterful Bible studies on the whole of Acts.

E.F. Harrison, *Interpreting Acts*, Academie, 1975.
An easy-to-read chapter-by-chapter discussion of Acts.

Useful general discussions of the history of the early church and of Lucan theology

C. Hemer, *The Book of Acts in the setting of Hellenistic History*, Mohr, 1989.
The most detailed and up-to-date study, confirming the historical reliability of the book of Acts.

H.C. Kee, *Good News to the Ends of the Earth: The Theology of Acts*, SCM, 1990.
A brilliant short study of the history and theology of Acts.

R. Maddox, *The Purpose of Luke — Acts*, T. & T. Clark, 1982.
The best scholarly general introduction to Lucan thought available.

I.H. Marshall, *Luke: Historian and Theologian*, Paternoster, 1970.
One of the earliest responses to Conzelmann, giving a

balanced overview of Luke's concerns.

Useful studies of specific issues touched on in this book which have contemporary relevance

❏ ASCENSION

K.N. Giles, 'The Ascension', in *The Dictionary of Christ and the Gospels*, IVP, 1992.
An essay mainly about Luke's understanding of the ascension, an event which came forty days after Christ's resurrection and exaltation.

❏ BREAKING OF BREAD/THE LORD'S SUPPER

I.H. Marshall, *Last Supper/Lord's Supper*, Paternoster, 1980.
A scholarly and clear summary of the biblical material on this topic.

❏ COMMUNITY OF GOODS

H.C. Kee, *Good News to the Ends of the Earth*, cited above, pp. 86 to 89.
A good brief discussion on the Christian communalism seen in the early chapters of Acts.

❏ CHURCH

H.C. Kee, *Good News to the Ends of the Earth*, cited above, pages 81 to 86.
A good discussion on the collective titles used of Christians in Acts.

G. Twelftree, *People of the Spirit*, Lancer, 1992.
Discusses Luke's understanding of the church. It is an

easy-to-read paperback.

❏ CHURCHES IN HOMES

R.J. Banks, *Going to Church in the First Century*, Hexagon, 1980.
A discussion of what took place when the early Christians gathered in a home for church.

Robert and Julia Banks, *The Church Comes Home*, Albatross, 1989.
An outline of the biblical evidence for home churches and of their operation today.

V. Branick, *The House Churches in the Writings of St Paul*, M. Glazier, 1989.
A scholarly study of the evidence.

❏ ESCHATOLOGY/THE LAST DAYS

K.N. Giles, 'Present—Future Eschatology in the Book of Acts', *Reformed Theological Review*, Vols 40 and 41, 1981, 1982, pp. 65 to 71 and 11 to 18.
A scholarly discussion of Luke's emphasis on the changed world brought about by Christ's death and resurrection.

❏ EVANGELISM

M. Green, *Evangelism in the Early Church*, Hodder and Stoughton, 1970.
A detailed account of evangelism in the early decades of Christian history. A book well worth reading.

❑ HOLY SPIRIT

K.N. Foster, *I Believe in Tongues: A Third View of the Charismatic Phenomenon*, Bethany, 1975.
A sane and sensible case for accepting tongue-speaking as a genuine gift.

❑ LEADERSHIP/MINISTRY

K.N. Giles, *Patterns of Ministry Among the First Christians*, Collins/Dove, 1989 and Harper and Row, 1990.
A study of how church leadership developed, with chapters on apostles, teachers, prophets elders and ordination.

H.C. Kee, *Good News to the Ends of the Earth*, cited above, pp. 70 to 81.
A brief, non-dogmatic discussion on the forms of Christian leadership seen in Acts.

❑ SALVATION

I.H. Marshall, *Luke: Historian and Theologian*, cited above, pp. 116 to 156.
Professor Marshall cogently argues that salvation is the main theme in Luke–Acts.

K.N. Giles, 'Salvation in Lucan Theology', *Reformed Theological Review*, Vols 41 and 42, 1983, pp.1 to 16 and 45 to 49.
A scholarly discussion of Luke's understanding of salvation.

❑ WOMEN

K.N. Giles, *Created Women*, Acorn, 1985.
A positive evaluation of the biblical teaching on the status and roles of women which discusses briefly why the

twelve apostles were all men and the ministry of women in Acts.

B. Witherington, *Women in the Earliest Churches*, CUP, 1988, pp. 128 to 157.
The best scholarly survey of what the New Testament says about women, with an excellent coverage of Luke's thought on the pages listed.

❑ SIGNS AND WONDERS/MIRACLES

H.W. Frost, *Miraculous Healing: A Personal Testimony and Biblical Study*, Evangelical Press, 1972.
Possibly the best little book on this contentious subject. Dr Frost affirms that God can and still does miraculously heal physical ills but he argues that God often allows those full of faith and love to suffer sickness and sometimes die early.

R.F. Gardiner, *Healing Miracles*, Darton, Longman and Todd, 1986.
A specialist doctor documents proven miraculous, physical healings.

John Goldingay (ed.), *Signs, Wonders and Healings*, IVP, 1989.
This book is in the series, 'When Christians Disagree'. The book presents a debate between the two main prevailing views on healing in today's church.

G.W.H. Lampe, 'Miracles in the Acts of the Apostles', in C.F.D. Moule (ed.), *Miracles*, Mowbray 1965.
A scholarly discussion of signs and wonders in Acts.